SPEAK
TO WIN

SPEAK
TO WIN

Georgiana Peacher, Ph.D.

BELL PUBLISHING COMPANY
NEW YORK

This 1985 edition is published by Bell Publishing Company, distributed by Crown Publishers, Inc., by arrange-
ment with Frederick Fell Publishers, Inc.

Printed and bound in the United States of America
Library of Congress Cataloging-in-Publication Data

Peacher, Georgiana.
   Speak to win.

   Reprint. Originally published: New York : F. Fell, 1966.
   Bibliography: p.
   1. Voice culture.   I. Title.
PN4162.P38   1985   808.5   85-15017
ISBN 0-517-47317-8

h g f e d c b

*This book is dedicated to
my patients and students*

Contents

Foreword

After reviewing Dr. Georgiana Peacher's manuscript on the mechanism of voice production in both health and disease, I am convinced that a perusal of her book will be of great value to both the doctor and the patient.

Attention to the fundamentals laid down by Dr. Peacher will aid in the prevention of problems related to voice production as well as aid in the rehabilitation of those who have acquired voice problems.

JAMES A. MOORE, M.D.
Professor Emeritus
Department of Otolaryngology
The New York Hospital

Preface

The past two decades have seen a remarkable advance in understanding of the mechanism of human voice production. With the techniques of high-speed cinephotography of the larynx, stroboscopic examination of the larynx, and basic researches involving electrical stimulation of individual muscles and muscle groups of the larynx, the action of the vocal cords is now better understood than ever before.

The laryngologist, the voice physiologist and the voice therapist have joined forces in studying the factors which are responsible for a voice of poor quality. In the professional voice user, such considerations may be of great importance in shaping a successful career. An even greater problem exists in those patients who have, through faulty voice use, developed a localized abnormality which may require both local treatment by the laryngologist and re-education of the speaking voice by the voice therapist.

Doctor Peacher's book is a practical aid in achieving the goals of voice therapy. In providing a background of information, presented in a readable and easily understood fashion, much will be contributed to the proper orientation of the patient who is about to undergo or who is already engaged in voice therapy. It will be especially useful to those who, for geographic reasons or lack of time, find it impossible to work with a voice therapist as often as might be desired.

The methods and exercises described by Doctor Peacher will no doubt also be helpful to speech therapists and laryngologists.

CHARLES M. NORRIS, M.D.
Former Chairman,
Department of Laryngology and
Broncho-Esophagology,
Chevalier Jackson Clinic,
Temple University,
Philadelphia

Acknowledgments

I wish to thank the following people:

DOCTOR O. SPURGEON ENGLISH, Professor and former Chairman of Psychiatry, Temple University Medical Center, who offered me an appointment in his department in 1948. He has given me inspiration and guidance throughout the years since.

DOCTOR LOUIS H. CLERF, Professor Emeritus and Chairman of Laryngology and Broncho-esophagology, Jefferson Medical School, who called me when I first came to Philadelphia and sent so many patients that I was forced to resign my full-time position to enter private practice in 1947.

The late distinguished DOCTOR CHEVALIER L. JACKSON, my former colleague at Temple, who was the first person to urge me to write this book.

DOCTOR PAUL H. HOLINGER, Professor of Broncho-esophagology, University of Illinois College of Medicine, who suggested my studying contact ulcer, supplied the patients for the study, and gave me much valuable aid and guidance.

I wish to thank Doctors JAMES A. MOORE and

CHARLES M. NORRIS for taking the time from their very busy schedules to write the Foreword and Preface. They have been particularly kind and helpful through the years, as have the following throat specialists: HIRAM A. ARMSTRONG, JOSEPH P. ATKINS, DANIEL C. BAKER, JR., WILLIAM H. BALTZELL, ARNOLD K. BRENMAN, JOHN F. DALY, MATTHEW S. ERSNER, LOUIS FRIEDMAN, FRED HARBERT, HERBERT P. HARKINS, LLOYD B. HARRISON, OTTO S. HENSLE, WILLIAM J. HITCHLER, HARVEY E. JORDAN, JR., ERNEST L. MCKENNA, JR., LAWRENCE J. MCSTRAVOG, EUGENE A. MEYER, DAVID MEYERS, HARRY R. MORSE, JOHN J. O'KEEFE, ROWAN C. PEARCE, F. JOHNSON PUTNEY, BERNARD J. RONIS, MAX RONIS, IRVING A. RUSH, JOSEPH SATALOFF, LOUIS E. SILCOX, JOSEPH G. SIRKEN, AUSTIN T. SMITH, GABRIEL T. TUCKER, JR., EMILY L. VAN LOON, and G. EDWARD ZERNE.

There have been many other physicians, psychiatrists, psychologists, and educators who have inspired and helped. Those psychiatrists who have been especially helpful are MORRIS W. BRODY, GEORGE DE CHERNEY, CALVIN S. DRAYER, HAROLD DILLON, HERBERT FREED, KALMAN FRANKEL, KENNETH H. GORDON, JR., BERYL JAFFE, ROBERT L. LEOPOLD, LEROY MAEDER, A. M. ORNSTEEN, MANUEL M. PEARSON, PAUL SLOANE, ELEANOR S. STEELE, HARRY WAGENHEIM, HELEN WAGENHEIM, and THOMAS S. WRIGHT.

DOCTOR CHARLES VAN RIPER, Director of the Speech Clinic at Western Michigan College, for his valuable criticism of the manuscript, which led me to revise it incorporating his excellent suggestions.

MISS SONIA LEVINTHAL, to whom I'm deeply indebted for her assistance in writing the book.

Miss Wanda Norstrom for her generosity in drawing the illustrations.

The late Professor Harry J. Heltman, who urged me to enter the School of Speech and Dramatic Art of Syracuse University, of which he was then head, and helped launch me into graduate study.

Doctors Clarence T. Simon and G. Paul Moore, my professors at Northwestern University who introduced me to vocal problems and directed my doctorate dissertation on contact ulcer of the larynx.

Mrs. Eulalia Garret Hewlett, my English teacher from the seventh to the tenth grades in the public schools of Syracuse, New York, who first encouraged me in writing.

Marietta Henry Massanisso and Anita Olachea for their secretarial help.

And very special thanks to the approximately two hundred speech therapists throughout the country who wrote asking me to write a practical book on voice.

SPEAK
TO WIN

Introduction

Your speaking voice is a powerful instrument in human relations. It is often the first yardstick by which other people measure your attractiveness —and even your ability.

Like a violin, your voice can be resonant and melodious, or it can sound weak or discordant and harsh. It can help you win the respect of your colleagues and subordinates, or it can be a factor in holding you back from positions of authority. Furthermore, you yourself are influenced by the sound of your own voice, and your confidence in yourself will be enhanced if it is firm, clear, and musical.

Very few people are endowed by nature with voices that enchant all who hear them. These are usually the result of attention and practice. You can give your voice this practice at home by spending no more time than you do shaving or caring for your hair or skin. It is within the power of almost every person to have a pleasing voice.

A normal voice, or what we call vocal maturity, has certain definite attributes:

1

1. Clearness
2. A natural pitch level according to one's age and sex
3. A flexible pitch range with use of melody and inflections
4. The easy attainment of loudness
5. The feeling of ease in the throat
6. A resonant quality
7. A normal rate with pauses
8. Free abdominal breathing
9. A slight vibrato
10. Continuous voicing

These are the qualities toward which we will aim in doing the exercises in this book. They should be done for five minutes every morning and for two to three minutes periodically throughout the day. After about eight to twelve weeks, only the morning practice will be necessary. You should continue this for at least six months or until your voice is completely re-educated and you are spontaneously using it in a correct and relaxed manner under all conditions. When you can do this, your voice will not only sound melodic, resonant, and clear even at increased volume, but you will also be safeguarding yourself against those physical diseases caused by misuse.

Your voice is one of your important assets. If you are in the entertainment world, its value is obvious, as evidenced by the drop in popularity of the silent screen's romantic heroes, Douglas Fairbanks and John Gilbert, who were heroes no more when sound came to the screen. Their voices were too high-pitched and lacked good tonal quality to fit their former roles. They looked the part but did not sound it.

A good voice is of utmost importance to everyone—especially to lawyers, ministers, teachers, lecturers, politicians, executives, and salesmen. In our everyday human relationships, it is also influential. For instance, our children from infancy on respond to the music in our voices. In a biography of Enrico Caruso, the author expresses beautifully the effect of voice:

> There is no medium for expressing sentiments or feelings so high, so strong, and so effective as to bear comparison with the human voice. Its power of impressiveness is uncommensurable, not only in relation to the significance of the words spoken, but at times even independent of them, when it lies wholly and intrinsically in the timbre and inflection of the voice itself. Its sound is the first to strike our ears, and to arouse our interest, which is attracted principally by its color and quality, independent of the contents of the words. That explains why certain great artists—Tommaso Salivni, for instance, or Sarah Bernhardt, or Eleanora Duse, and even the celebrated Yvette Gilbert—conquered the world, after performing for audiences who were not even familiar with their languages, but were deeply affected by the accent, the clarity, the beauty,

the pathos, and musical color of the timbre of
their voices.*

There is still another and even more powerful incentive for improving your voice. The same
exercises that make your voice melodious and pleasant will, even more importantly, help prevent
polyps, nodules, and contact ulcers of the vocal
cords. Often polyps, nodules, thickening, and contact ulcers of the vocal cords actually disappear when
the voice is re-educated by the proper exercise.

I have therefore written this book about
practical vocal improvement for those who wish
simply to make their voices sound better for business or personal reasons and for those who have
definite problems like hoarseness, weakness, or loss
of voice, and vocal fatigue. I have had many re-
quests from speech therapists throughout the country to write such a book.

My book should be especially helpful to
those who have or have had vocal nodules, polyps,
or contact ulcers on their vocal cords. These conditions and some others come from abuses which
can be eliminated by vocal therapy and by doing
the exercises described in this book. Of course, in
some cases, the patient must have an operation first,
and a throat specialist must be consulted in all of
these conditions. For those who have or have had
trouble, it would be more helpful if they used
this book with a speech therapist, if possible. And

* From *Caruso's Method of Voice Production* by Mario
P. Marafioti, New York, Appleton-Century-Crofts, 1950.

I cannot say strongly enough that it is absolutely essential in any instance of hoarseness lasting more than two weeks to consult a throat specialist. In fact, I always insist that a patient with hoarseness consult a laryngologist before I offer any treatment.

Parents, kindergarten and grade-school teachers, speech teachers, and speech therapists may use this book with children. When I work with children I use basically the same exercises and practice plans, making games of them to keep them interested. For instance, in the first exercise of a list of words beginning with the sound "h," I quickly bring out a stack of cards and colored magic markers or crayolas and a spinner, and we begin a game. Simple pictures are easy to make and children love to make some of their own. By the end of the game one of us has won and the child has a batch of "h" pictures to take home to play with every day. Besides, the child may search magazines for horses, houses, hats, hoops, and other "h" pictures to add to his game or for a scrapbook. Children like to match pictures, too, and play the "Old Maid" type of game, when two pictures of a kind are used. There are countless varieties of games to which one can adapt the exercises. Instead of reading the adult poems, children enjoy jingles like "Robin the Bobbin, the Big-Bellied Ben."

I hope my book will be helpful also to speech therapists for use with their patients, and I hope laryngologists will recommend it to their patients, especially in those localities where a qualified therapist of the American Speech and Hearing Association is not available. It may be used also as a practical drill book in college, speech classes, high schools, music schools, theological seminaries, teachers' colleges and business schools.

There are other speech problems with which I work, namely, aphasia, stuttering, cleft palate, diction, cerebral palsy, and hearing difficulty. Certain chapters in my book may help three of these categories: those who have stuttering, cleft palate, or are hard of hearing, even though these three conditions do need more than these exercises alone.

Chapter I

How Your Voice Works

The voice is produced in the larynx, which houses and protects the vocal cords. The larynx itself is an enlargement of the tube from the mouth to the lungs. It is a rigid tube of movable parts, composed of cartilages, muscles, ligaments, and membrane. You may find your larynx by feeling the middle part of the front of your throat below your chin. In some men, you can see the larynx protrude and move up and down. Figure I shows a movable mechanical model of the larynx. The largest cartilage seen is the thyroid cartilage.

The larynx has another function besides producing voice. It acts as a valve which closes to keep the air in your lungs when you lift something heavy, swing a golf club, or run a race. It is this action which sometimes causes athletes' voices to become hoarse or weak after strenuous exertion.

There are nine cartilages in the larynx itself and a tenth above the larynx from which it is suspended.

The vocal cords were so called long before anatomical dissections and before it was possible

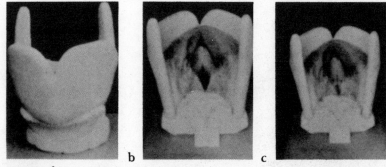

a   b   c

FIGURE 1.

Mechanical Model of the Larynx. Front view (a). Back view (b) showing vocal cords apart and at rest. Back view (c) with vocal cords together and vibrating.

to see them distinctly. It was generally believed that they were cords similar to those on a harpsichord and similar musical instruments. Now we know that they are not cords at all, but folds of mucous membrane covering the inner surface of the larynx.

These folds run from front to back. They are joined in the front and are apart in the back when we are not talking, looking like a triangle when viewed from above. This is what the throat specialist sees when he looks at your vocal cords with a mirror. (See Figure 2.)

When we talk, the back of the vocal cords come together and vibrate, thus producing voice. The pitch of your voice determines the number of vibrations per second. The higher the pitch, the more vibrations. For instance, at middle C there are 256 vibrations per second. At the high C, two octaves above middle C, there are 1,024 vibrations per second.

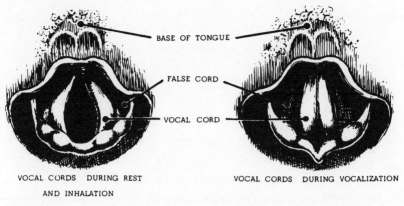

VOCAL CORDS DURING REST
AND INHALATION

VOCAL CORDS DURING VOCALIZATION

FIGURE 2.

The vocal cords are attached in back to two small cartilages, the arytenoids. In the front they are attached to the inside of the thyroid cartilage. The arytenoid cartilages go through many complex movements. When they come together they bring the vocal cords together to produce voice. In doing this they slide upward, they rotate inward, and each slides toward the midline. In bringing the vocal folds apart, they go in opposite directions. While we speak correctly they should come together and remain in one position during the vibrations.

There are many muscles in the larynx and two nerves which activate phonation.

So it is in the larynx that the voice is produced. However, if we did not have the structures above the larynx, namely, the pharyngeal cavity (the space above the larynx which continues up to the nose), the nose, and the mouth, we would produce only a very weak, thin squeak. It would be like blowing on just the mouthpiece of a bugle.

As the vibrations come up from the larynx, the tone is expanded, amplified, and resonated in the upper cavities. Resonance is simply the amplification and variation of the tone as it is sent from the vocal cords up to these resonators, and adding resonance to your voice means having some of the air pass through the nose and thus adding nasality. If we have too much resonance, however, we have an excessively nasal voice. We must have just enough. The humming exercises in this book will help you improve the resonance of your voice without becoming overresonant or nasal.

Besides the larynx, the resonators, and central nervous system control, we must have the breath, which comes up below to move the vocal cords into vibration. The breathing apparatus consists of the lungs; the muscles of the abdomen, which can control the rate at which the air is expired; the rib cage; and many other muscles and nerves. The air channel begins at the mouth and nose, runs down through the larynx, trachea, and into the lower parts of the lungs.

The bottom of the chest cavity is formed by a smooth muscle called the diaphragm. It is simply a sheaf of muscle which divides the thoracic from the abdominal cavity. Above it are the heart and lungs, and below it is the abdominal cavity. When we breathe we expand the abdominal area. This is called abdominal breathing. We talk normally only during exhalation, i.e., while the breath is passing through the vocal cords. The chapter on breathing will explain this in detail.

Though there has been much talk of the voice since the writing on Egyptian papyrus five thousand years ago, the scientific study of the voice has only been going on for around fifty years. New methods are constantly being discovered. The future will bring much more knowledge about the voice and how it works.

Chapter II

Six Simple Rules Everyone Should Follow

There are certain general measures each of us should take to keep the voice healthy and develop its pleasant qualities. They are simple rules which will help keep your voice good and strong and guard it from physical abuse. Try following these six simple suggestions and you will be rewarded by a healthier, stronger, and more attractive voice.

1. Always keep your head straight when you talk. Remember this especially when talking on the telephone. Mothers and fathers should be careful when they read aloud to their children; and clubwomen, lawyers, politicians, clergymen, and teachers should remember this when they make speeches from prepared notes. The reason is that when you talk, the larynx rises. Therefore, if you bend your head down or to one side, you press against your larynx as it moves up. This constricted position also interferes with proper breathing and causes great tension.

There are always ways to keep your head straight while talking. When you make a speech hold your notes up on a lectern. If this isn't possible, glance down at them. Then straighten up before you begin your speech. Even in the unusual instance of the Broadway actor who played the drunk in a play and had to roll his head around while speaking, we managed to correct his problem by a simple device. He created the illusion of rolling his head around while talking by doing this only when someone else held the stage. During his own lines, he kept his head erect.

2. Always give your abdomen the freedom to move. A tight belt or girdle will interfere with abdominal breathing, which is necessary for easy vocal use. Also, wear a loose collar that doesn't press on the larynx. Eating too much hinders this free breathing, so eat lightly if you have to make a long speech.

3. Instead of clearing your throat or coughing, try swallowing, pausing, or taking a deep breath. If you can't avoid clearing your throat, do it as gently as possible and without voice, particularly if you already have trouble with your voice.

4. Try to keep your mouth closed when you are out in cold or damp air. When you must speak, be sure you open your mouth wide enough, because clamping the teeth creates tension.

5. Avoid talking too much when you're over-tired, when your throat is dry, or when you're hungry. And if you know you're under severe emotional strain, try to cut down on your conversation

a bit. You should also avoid talking too much after you've had a few drinks, for your larynx becomes desensitized and you're apt to misuse your voice because it sounds and feels better. This is an illusion in much the same way that seeming benefits from lozenges, gargles, and sprays are. These, incidentally, should be used only for specific infections.

6. When you have to talk above constant noise, in the subway, in a car, or simply in the street, try to rest your voice frequently. And if you work in a factory, in a department store, around airplanes, or other noisy places, you should rest your voice at some period during the day or evening to counteract the strain. If you play golf all day, shouting around the course, go back to the clubhouse and rest your voice awhile. Singers certainly should be very careful to rest their voices. For instance, it is a wise precaution for a singer to avoid any talking whatever during the day if he or she is going to sing that evening.

Chapter III

The First Step: How to Relax
Your Voice Muscles

When you are tense, the muscles of your larynx become tense. Most people with vocal problems notice an increase in symptoms when they are emotionally upset or under pressure. However, you can learn to relax your voice muscles and keep them relaxed, even when you are under pressure or emotionally upset. If you find that, under severe stress, you can't relax, avoid talking as much as possible. The more tension you feel in the throat, the more often you should do the relaxing exercises in this chapter, to offset the effects of emotional tension on your larynx. Another important tip is to open your mouth wider when you speak. Never talk through clenched teeth.

The following exercises will help relax the external muscles of the throat as well as the small muscles of the larynx. Do at least one of these exercises before any other—before each vocal practice.

1. *Yawn:* Open the mouth wide, take a deep breath, and simulate an easy yawn. This is best for

the so-called open throat, which technically means relaxation of the laryngeal muscles with the vocal cords wide apart. Yawn at least five times. But don't produce too strenuous a yawn, as this increases tension.

2. *Rotation of the head:* Sit limply with arms hanging at the sides of a chair. Drop the head, turn toward one side, back as far as possible, to the opposite side and again down. Drop the jaw open in the back position, so as not to pull the frontal muscles of the neck. Rotate very slowly so that your head is hardly moving. More rapid rotation produces dizziness and does not aid relaxation. This exercise is best for the external muscles of the neck. Repeat five to ten times. If the back position is hard to obtain, drop the head downward only, and from side to side.

3. *Stand:* Bend forward and downward. Shake hands and arms from shoulders continuously; and at the same time, swing from waist to the left, and then to the right. Continue five to ten turns.

4. *Breathe:* Breathe in and out deeply, until you feel a relaxation of the vocal folds. The larynx can be tense even when the voice is not in use. This is termed subvocal speech. So it's a good idea to do this exercise once in a while when you're reading or watching TV.

5. *Shake your head* and let your jaw shake on its hinges.

6. *Say a few words* with your tongue forward. Be sure it isn't bunched in the back of your mouth.

7. *Open your mouth wide* and say the following:

hah, hah, hah, hah, hah

yah, yah, yah, yah, yah

wah, wah, wah, wah, wah

bah, bah, bah, bah, bah

kah, kah, kah, kah, kah

lah, lah, lah, lah, lah

pah, pah, pah, pah, pah

fah, fah, fah, fah, fah

vah, vah, vah, vah, vah

thah, thah, thah, thah

jah, jah, jah, jah, jah

sah, sah, sah, sah, sah

zah, zah, zah, zah, zah

shah, shah, shah, shah

tah, tah, tah, tah, tah

dah, dah, dah, dah, dah

rah, rah, rah, rah, rah

mah, mah, mah, mah, mah

nah, nah, nah, nah, nah

Chapter IV

How to Get Your Right Pitch

The proper pitch, or your optimum pitch, is the one at which your voice sounds clearest, feels easiest when you speak, and gives you the greatest amount of volume with the least amount of effort. It is this pitch around which you will build your voice. It is not difficult to find this optimum pitch. You will then do all the succeeding exercises in this book at your correct pitch, and after a while you will maintain this pitch spontaneously whenever you speak.

When you speak or sing in the correct or optimum pitch, you can avoid many future difficulties. Of course, you can learn to extend your pitch range, but it must be done correctly and carefully, as demonstrated in the chapter on melody.

The first step in getting your correct pitch is to go to the piano or other musical instrument and say, "How, How, How," in your natural voice. Then match this pitch on the instrument. This will be your used average pitch, but it will not necessarily be your best.

Then sing down from this used pitch to the lowest note you can reach, then sing up to the highest you can reach. This will be your total range. Experiment up and down around this used pitch and find the note that sounds the best, is the clearest, and gives you the greatest volume with the least effort. It will be a middle pitch rather than too low or too high. This will then be the optimum pitch from which you will build your voice.

If you find this difficult to do alone, ask a friend to listen to you, or use a recording machine. Naturally, it would be even better to have a vocal therapist help you find your right pitch, but you can do it alone.

Now that you have found your correct pitch, you will do all the exercises in this book at that correct pitch. If you want to remind yourself of the correct pitch, buy a pitch pipe or small xylophone in any music store and find your note on it. You will find that it will soon become spontaneous. The exercises in the chapter on resonance will be especially helpful in maintaining the right pitch.

Don't be surprised if you find you have to raise your pitch. Most people who have vocal problems will have to raise their pitch from two to five notes. This is contrary to the popular conception that a beautiful speaking voice is always low-pitched. Any number of patients who have raised their pitch several notes have told me that their friends have commented on their attractive voice by saying, "Your voice sounds beautiful. It's much lower, isn't it?" Most people just assume that when a voice is pleasant, melodious, and resonant, it is low-pitched. And the contrary is so often true. Most patients have had to raise their pitch, not lower it.

With hoarseness, the pitch automatically lowers to the lower part of one's vocal range. This is why pitch is so important in bringing a hoarse voice back to normal. Often, by speaking just somewhat higher in pitch, the hoarseness disappears immediately.

Many men are surprised when we tell them we want to raise their pitch. They're afraid of sounding feminine. Actually, when they speak at a higher pitch and increase their resonance, which improves the general quality of their voices, they sound more masculine. Franklin D. Roosevelt, for instance, sounded masculine enough even though he had a fairly high pitch for a man, simply because his voice was resonant and melodious.

What makes a voice sound feminine is not the pitch, as is shown by a homosexual patient; his voice was very high-pitched, but when we lowered it we found that it still sounded feminine—like a woman with a low-pitched voice—and people still called him "Miss" on the phone. Then we worked on melody and intonation, and he sounded much better. So it is really the type of melody pattern which determines whether a man will sound masculine or feminine.

Fashion sometimes dictates the pitch some women use. In recent years there has been a trend toward preference for a low-pitched voice. As a result, many women do irreparable harm to their voices by forcing their pitch downward in order to obtain what they think is a low, flattering tone.

Be careful that you don't lower your pitch inadvertently when for some reason you have to talk softly.

Often, in trying to disguise our voices by talking softly, without realizing it we are lowering our pitch too much. Actors sometimes get into trouble trying to talk softly between acts. And judges who have to talk to lawyers in court sometimes develop contact ulcers because of this. You can learn to disguise your voice, but you must keep your correct pitch. In watching the television program *What's My Line,* I've noticed that, when the mystery guest disguises his voice, he often ends up hoarse just because he's lowering his pitch.

Chapter V

How to Breathe Correctly
When You Speak or Sing

The best way to achieve easy breathing when you speak, although it can also be done by sitting and standing erect, is to lie on your back with a small pillow under your head. A large pillow pushes the head forward too much, and we have said before, your head should be straight when you speak. Lying down, you breathe abdominally; and if you do your exercises lying down, this abdominal breath-ing soon becomes habitual. Therefore, we recom-mend that at the beginning you do your exercises lying down as often as you possibly can, especially the first five-minute period of exercise in the morn-ing. During the day, you can do them while sitting erect at your desk or standing erect. Good posture is important.

The proper type of breathing, and that which gives the best breath control during speech, is easy breathing. Don't expel your breath too quickly. In other words, don't force expiration. This is most injurious to the vocal cords. For low or average volume, it is never necessary to push the breath. Just take the air into your lungs by filling the area around your abdomen, and let it come out naturally with the abdominal muscles relaxed. Later, you will learn how to increase your volume, in the chapter on getting greater volume.

The drawings will show you what happens when you breathe. (See Figure 3.) The abdominal area expands as breath enters the lungs, and goes down like a bellows as it leaves.

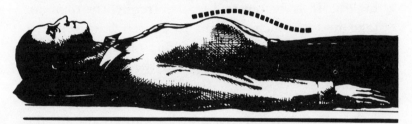

FIGURE 3.

Abdominal Breathing. The Abdominal area expands when you inhale, to a peak shown by the broken line. It goes down on exhalation. The position of the man's waist shows the end of exhalation

When you breathe without vocalizing, for instance when you are reading or taking a walk, you naturally breathe in through your nose. However, when you use your voice while talking or singing, this would not be natural and would take too long. Therefore, when you vocalize and when you do the exercises, you should breathe in through your mouth.

Take a deep breath through your mouth and fill the area all around your waist. The area around your waist should always expand when you breathe in. This is contrary to the way most of us are taught in the gym. There we are taught to throw our chest out when we inhale—this is called thoracic breathing. It is reverse breathing and it is incorrect. After you take your deep breath and feel the abdominal expansion, you bring your stomach in and vocalize as the air comes out. This should be done slowly and easily. Do all the exercises in the book in a moderate voice with these slow and easy breaths.

Be sure you take in enough air when you breathe. However, don't pack your lungs with breath. It is better to breathe frequently than to take in too much air and to go too long on one breath. When you speak too long on one breath, a point is reached beyond which the voice becomes strained.

To get this better breath control, stand erect with your arms relaxed at your side. Take in air slowly through your nose and without straining. Feel the abdominal area expand. Then let the air out slowly by gently pulling in your abdominal muscles.

As we have said, don't wear too tight clothing and don't overeat, as these interfere with breathing.

"Phrasing" means taking breaths according to the phrases or clauses in a sentence. People with vocal problems tend to go too long on a breath.

Anyone can be trained or can train himself to go a long way on one breath and use most of the air in the lungs, but we should use only up to 25 per cent of the air in the lungs for speaking. If we go beyond this, we are using supplemental air. Around 75 per cent of the lung capacity should remain in the lungs at all times.

Try speaking as long as you can on a breath, and you will reach a point where you can still speak if you keep squeezing the air out, but this squeezing results in increasing muscle tension in the larynx. So. take more frequent breaths as you speak, and pattern them according to the phrases. Then you will not go beyond your limit.

Speak the following poem in a low conversational level of volume. Open your mouth wide and breathe in at each slash mark. This will help form the habit of breathing more often with control of the breath.

Since this is your first exercise, it is a good time to remind you that vocal exercises should be done for only five minutes at one time. Do them slowly and carefully rather than trying to do a lot at once. Try to spend five minutes doing the exercises the first thing in the morning and then try to spend a few minutes every hour during the day. We recommend a total of at least a half-hour a day, but ideally you should try to do them for two to three minutes every hour.

Speak the poem which follows in average conversational level of volume. When not using the voice, breathe through your nose. Here you begin using your voice and now breathe through your mouth. It is not natural and takes too long to take the breath in through your nose while talking or

singing. Open wide and breathe in at each slanting
mark. This will help form the habit of breathing
more often with control of the breath.

"Beginning My Studies," by Walt Whitman.

/ Beginning my studies / the first step pleased me so
    much,
/ The mere fact / consciousness, / these forms, / the
    power of motion,
/ The least insect or animal, / the senses, / eyesight,
    / love,
/ The first step / I say / awed me / and pleas'd me so
    much,
/ I have hardly gone / and hardly wish'd / to go any
    farther,
/ But stop / and loiter all the time / to sing it / in
    ecstatic songs.

Say this poem in the same way, breathing in
at each mark.

"Reeds of Innocence," by William Blake.

/ Piping down the valleys wild,
/ Piping songs of pleasant glee,
/ On a cloud / I saw a child,
/ And he laughing / said to me:

/ "Pipe a song about a lamb!"
/ So I piped with merry cheer.
/ "Piper, / pipe that song again;"
/ So I piped: / he wept to hear.

/ "Drop thy pipe, / thy happy pipe;
/ Sing thy songs of happy cheer!"
/ So I sung the same again,
/ While he wept with joy to hear.

/ "Piper, sit thee down / and write
   In a book / that all may read."
/ So he vanish'd from my sight;
/ And I pluck'd a hollow reed,

/ And I made a rural pen,
/ And I stain'd the water clear,
/ And I wrote my happy songs
/ Every child may joy to hear.

Chapter VI

The Easy Initiation of Voice

The easy initiation of voice is a vital factor in making your voice sound pleasing by improving the timbre, and it is especially important for the health of your voice. By easy initiation of voice, we mean that in those words starting with a vowel or a sound like "m" or "n," we initiate the tone gently, slipping into it easily and safely. This will protect your vocal cords because you will be bringing them together tenderly and gently instead of banging them together harshly.

The exercises in this chapter will teach you how to initiate tone easily.

You will spend the next week or two doing just the exercises in this chapter. Note that all these words begin with "h." The reason for this is that the "h" before the vowel helps you initiate easily.

Every morning for the next week or two, spend five minutes when you get up, doing just the exercises to follow—those words beginning with "h." Do them lying down to help you get in the practice of breathing correctly. Place a small pillow under your head. Don't forget to do a few relaxing exercises first. You must also do them at your correct pitch. Blow your pitch pipe or play the note on your piano to remind yourself of your optimum pitch.

During the day, try to do them for a minute or two at your desk every once in a while. To repeat—always remember to:

1. Do a few relaxing exercises first.

2. Say the words at your optimum pitch. Blow your pitch pipe frequently to remind you of your correct pitch.

3. Open your mouth as wide as possible on each word.

4. Take a breath through your mouth on each word by expanding your abdominal cavity. Then say the word as you expel the air by gently pulling your stomach in.

how	hill	hood	whose	ham
hay	hall	hold	house	him
high	howl	head	horse	hum
hoe	whole	hock	hiss	home
who	heat	hike	haze	hearth
haw	hot	hook	hape	hang
he	hut	hug	hip	hung
hoy	hat	hog	hoop	hitch
her	hit	have	hop	hatch
huh	hoot	heave	hope	hunch
here	had	hive	hub	hinge
hair	hid	has	huff	help
hail	hide	his	hoof	hard
heel	heard	hose	hand	hack

Hague	harsh	heap	hest	halt
hake	heart	heath	height	hone
half	hasp	heed	hilt	honk
Hals	haste	heel	hinge	hooch
halt	hast	helm	hint	horn
Han	hate	hem	hire	host
hap	hath	helve	hist	hound
hare	haul	hemp	hoax	hove
hark	haunch	her	hob	hue
harm	haunt	hence	hod	huge
harp	hawed	hurl	hoist	hull
hush	hawk	Herm	hom	hulk
hash	hawse	hers	Holmes	Hume

You now have spent one to two weeks practicing words beginning with "h." You are now
ready to transfer what you have learned to words
that don't begin with "h." You should now be
bringing your cords together gently, and initiating
tone more easily. For the next week, do the exercises in the rest of this chapter. Again we remind
you:

1. Do a few relaxing exercises first.

2. Be sure you stay on the correct pitch.

3. Open your mouth as wide as possible on
each word, as you get the most relaxation in your
throat this way.

4. Take a separate breath on each word. For
instance, take one on "ha" and a new one on "ah,"
a separate one on "harbor," and a new one on
"arbor." If the vowels do not come easily, try yawn-
ing between each word. Open your mouth wide,

simulate an easy yawn, and on the yawn, say the word. Do not wait to get set after you take the new breath, as this is a sure way to hit hard. Say the word beginning with the vowel at the peak of inspiration, so to speak.

You will find that, after saying "ha," you will now be able to say "ah" easier without banging your vocal cords together too hard. Some people find that they can gain the easy initiation of tone more effectively by saying the word beginning with the vowel at a slightly higher pitch. For instance, the word "ha" would be said at optimum pitch, and the "ah" would be said one or two notes higher. Remember, don't do the exercises for more than five minutes at a time, and try to do a few relaxing exercises first.

ha - ah	harm - arm
harbor - arbor	harmful - armful
Harvey - Arvey	Hartz - arts
Harleigh - Arleigh	hod - odd
Haarlen - Arlen	holla - allah
Harnold - Arnold	holly - Ollie
hearth - Arthur	harms - arms
heart - art	haha - aha
hark - ark	Hoffritz - ahfritz
harden - Arden	honk - onk
high - I	Highs - eyes
hike - Ike	hire - ire
heil - I'll	hide - I'd
hive - I've	highland - island

highs - ice   high fly - I fly
Higham - I'm   highland - I land
hides - ides   high light - I light
Hibernia - Ibernia   high pitch - I pitch
hibiscus - ibex   Haile - ilex
high-brow - eye brow   Hayakawa - I'll see you

how - ow   Howes - ows
howl - owl   hound - our
house - oust   houses - ousted
how - out   housework - outwork
how's - ounce   houseless - Oursler
how - outdoors   howlet - Oundle
how - outings   Housman - outcome
Howell - Owell   Haugen - Auer

haw - awe   horn - ornament
hall - all   Hornell - orphan
hawk - awkward   Horner - orphrey
halt - altar   hornet - orris
Hawthorne - author   horrible - Orpheus
hauberk - auburn   hallways - always
haught - ought   Hallcott - Alcott
haul - awl   Haldane - Aulden
Haugen - auger   hallmark - all marks
hoar - oar   horrid - orange
Horby - orby

hoy - oy   hoi - ointment
hoil - oil   hoil - oilcloth
Hoyer - oyer   hoil - oil proof
hoy - oyster   hoil - oil skin

hoil - oil stone

hoyed - oiled

hoyden - oilless

hoydened - oily

hoydening - oilproof paint

hunh - uh

hump - umph

huckle - uncle

hug - ugh

hull - ull

hulk - ultra

hum - umm

hunter - under

hup - up

hunk - unk

hovel - oven

hunger - onion

Humber - umber

Hun - un

humble - umbel

humblebee - umbellate

humbug - umbles

Humboldt - umbra

Humphrey - umbrella

hunch - unch

hung - unction

hunted - untilled

Huntington - untold

Hutton - utter

husk - usk

Huss - us

Huxley - Uxbridge

Hupmobile - umpire

had - add

hack - act

ham - am

haft - aft

hand - and

hat - at

has - as

hash - ash

Hal - Al

Han - an

Hants - ants

Hasp - asp

habit - abbey

hackle - ankle

hackney - acme

Haddington - Addington

Hansen - Anson

Haensel - ancillary

Hansel - answer

Halley - alley

Hallem - alum

Halleck - Alec

hamper - ampere

Hamsun - Amson

handy - Andy

hangar - angle

hanker - anchor

harrier - airier

Hannah - Anna

harrow - arrow

Hattie - attic

hashish - ashes

Hannibal - Annabelle

Habana - Abana

Harun - Aaron

habit - Abbott

hair - air

heavy - Evie

hen - N

Hecht - ectoplasm

hell - el

hex - ecstasy

Hess - S

heckle - Eckle

hex - x

hectic - eclectic

hedge - edge

Hector - Ecuador

head - Ed

Hegel - Egbert

held - eld

Hellene - Eline

heft - eft

Herrick - Eric

hem - Em

Hesper - esker

helm - elm

Hester - Esther

Hetch - etch

Heddy - Eddy

helk - elk

Hedda - Edda

Harry - airy

heron - Aaron

Helen - Ellen

Heston - Eston

hairbrush - airbrush

Harritt - arid

heron - Erin

hay - A

hate - aid

hate - ate

Haise - ace

haze - A's

Hadrian - Adrian

hake - ache

Haiti - eighty

hail - ail

Hayden - Ayden

hape - ape

Hades - aids

hame - aim

Hague - ague

hale - ale

hailstorm - Alestorm

hasten - aces　　　　　hasty - acre
Hastings - asynchronous　Haverhill - Averill

her - err　　　　　hermit - Urquhart
herd - erg　　　　　Herder - Ursa
hurl - Earl　　　　　Hercules - Ursa Major
heard - earth　　　　　Herkimer - Ursula
hers - errs　　　　　herself - Urswick
herd - earth　　　　　herdsman - urban
Hurleigh - early　　　　　Herschel - urbanite
Herman - ermine　　　　　Herbert - herbage
Herma - Erma

hurrah - around　　　　　Hawaii - away
hurrah - array　　　　　habilitate - abide
huzza - upon　　　　　habitual - ability
habitual - about　　　　　Hawarden - a warden
hallo - allow

how - oh　　　　　Holden - olden
hose - o's　　　　　Houghton - oughton
home - ohm　　　　　holster - Olster
hold - old　　　　　hobo - oboe
hold - ole　　　　　holder - older
Holm - olm　　　　　holy - Olie
hoax - oaks　　　　　hocum - oakum
hone - own　　　　　Homer - omer
hoed - ode　　　　　hotel - Othello
hautboy - oh boy　　　　　hostess - Osler

hood - umlaut　　　　　hooch - ooch
hook - umlauted　　　　　hood - ood

hoof - oof
hook - ook
hookah - ookah
hooky - ooky
hoop - oop
hoopee - oopee
hooray - ooray
Hoosac - oosac
Hultzen - Urdu

Humperdinck -
        Umperdinck
hussar - ussar
hoodman - oodman
hoodwink - oodwink
hooked - ooked
Hooker - ooker
hookup - ookup
hood - oody

who - oo
whose - ooze
who - uhlan
hooch - uhland
whom - umiak
hoodlum - Unalaska
hoodoo - oolong

who'll - Oona
Hugli - oozy
hooey - oolah
whoe'er - oomiak
Hooghly - oozed
whose - oozes

his - is
hit - it
hitch - itch
here - ear
hid - id
hill - ill
hint - ink
hinge -inch
hears - ears

hits - its
him - in
Hilda - Ilda
hearing - earring
Hindu - into
Hyksos - Iksos
hypnosis - Ippie
hymnal - Immie

he - E
heat - eat
heave - eve
heel - eel

heeds - Eads
he's - ease
heating - eating
heath - Ethan

heathen - Ethan   Hera - era
heathen - either   Here - Erie
Heavener - evener   heathen - even
Hebe - Eby   heatable - eatable

This breathy approach that you have now become accustomed to using will help initiate voice easily. You should now, after a few weeks of these exercises, be initiating voice more easily. When you feel that you have established the habit of easy beginning, stop doing the "h's" so that your tone doesn't become too breathy. If you should find that you again have trouble, go back to the "h's" for a short period. The exercises on blending in the next chapter will also help you avoid hitting your vocal cords together too hard.

Chapter VII

The Second Step: Learn How to Blend Your Words

You have now learned how to initiate tone easily. The next step is to learn how to blend words into vowels so that you do not have to initiate voice on every single vowel word. You do this by blending your consonants into words that begin with vowels. This is proper English usage, and it helps you not only to avoid physical problems but makes your voice pleasanter and more musical. You should do this in singing, too.

Blending is not slurring or sloppy speaking. As we said, it is simply attaching the final consonant or vowel of the first word to the initial vowel of the following word. Take the words "sit upon," for instance. You should blend the "t" of sit into the "u" of upon, without pausing after sit and then hitting hard on the "u" of upon. If you say "tapon" and then "sit‿upon," attaching the "t" to the "u," then you are blending. This makes it impossible for you to begin the "u" in any other manner than gently. Special exercises follow, making it easy for you to learn how to blend. For "sit upon," for instance, say "tapon," and then "si-tapon," and then "sit upon"—and you will be on your way.

These exercises will teach you how to blend your words. Do them at your optimum pitch. Take a breath with each new phrase. Breathe in through the mouth and expand the abdominal cavity. Say the phrase on the outgoing breath as you bring in your abdominal muscles.

see‿it	freeze‿up	lag‿along
if‿I	camouflage‿on	sing‿out
believe‿I	flash‿out	wander‿about
come‿in	jet‿airplane	country‿is
pipe‿of	wade‿in	hang‿up
Bob‿is	shall‿I	can‿of
he‿is	car‿is	see‿Eva
they‿are	win‿it	Kay‿is
watch‿over	how‿are	high‿up
judge‿it	see‿over	so—I
bus‿and	you‿are	Lou‿and
lose‿it	back‿of	who‿are
speech‿obscure	rose‿against	Hugh‿obtained
many‿arts	yet‿another	the‿earth
now‿are	that‿all	speak‿out
he‿attains	my‿own	of‿early
nor‿ever	shall‿utter	some‿other
the‿onlookers	can‿avail	of‿us
seeing‿eye	search‿out	look‿upon
the‿ocean	will‿ask	best‿advise

"H" sentences are given next to help easy adduction of the vocal cords. The connecting mark "‿" is used to indicate where words may be blended into vowels. Speak these naturally as close to your optimum pitch as you can.

Take as many breaths as you need. Remember to breathe in through your mouth and expand the abdominal cavity.

Say each phrase on the outgoing breath as you slowly pull in your abdominal muscles.

If you happen to take a breath at a blending mark, be sure you indicate tone easily on that vowel.

How⌣are you?

Have you had dinner?

Helen⌣is⌣over by the river.

Hail⌣and hear his speech.

Hold⌣onto the reins.

Haitians have⌣a unique⌣art⌣assembled with tin cans.

Henry⌣is⌣at home.

Has⌣Ellen been⌣around today?

His⌣uncle was⌣in⌣India.

Help the children to read.

Here⌣are Elizabeth⌣and⌣Edmund.

Hide⌣in the cupboard.

Hillary⌣is bicycling⌣on the plains.

Habits⌣are made by repetitive usage.

Hurry⌣up the hills⌣of⌣Harrisburg.

Hammocks swung⌣in the wispy breezes.

Hazy⌣overcasts⌣of shadows were seen.

Hollyhocks surrounded Lulu's yellow house.

Hugo led his sheep⌣into the pasture.

Begin easily on each new breath and blend into initial vowels. Initial "h" words are used to give the feeling of beginning gently on each new breath and prevent irritation to the vocal cords.

Hawe's Hut
Hug House
he - hippos
happy hills
husky hush
hunt hyenas
hoopla hoops
happy Hannah
hanging
  hampers
husky hushing
high heap
Harry Hark
horses' hoofs
hundred Huns
his horn
haphazard hat
haunted horses
highland height
hunting and
  haunting
hungry
  hummingbird
hinder‿and
  harass
Harry's hatchet
hair‿off her
  head
half‿ahead
hamper‿and

harm
hot‿and
  humdrum
hallooing
Harold
heaps‿of horses
Horatio‿and
  Horatius
hunt the
  haddock
houses‿on hills
hopeless
  huntsman
hooting hawks
Higgens the
  higgler
hearts‿of
  herons
hand‿in hand
He held his
  handkerchief.
He happens to
  have‿a harp.
He had heard
  him.
He had‿a
  hoarse horse.
Who heard his
  hiss?
He had hooked

hams.
Hatta held her
  hand for hay.
He heard Harry
  hurry.
Hills‿are
  higher‿in
  Hawaii.
Hear his hungry
  cry.
Herman held
  his head high.
Hardheads have
  heartaches.
"Hello," hailed
  the hunter.
He hummed the
  hymn.
How have you
  hurt him?
Hasten‿and
  heal his hand.
Hairbreath
  Harry held
  his head.
Helga had
  hundreds‿of
  hogs.

Begin with ease on the first word of each
sentence and blend into the other initial vowels at

the blending marks. Remember, if you have to take
a breath at a blending mark, initiate tone easily.
Keep around your optimum pitch. Do a few relaxing exercises first and never practice more than five
minutes at a time.

I think so.

I don't mean that.

Oh, that's nonsense!

Of course⌣Edmund⌣is
  here.

I⌣am quite⌣aware⌣
  of⌣it.

It's rather nice.

I believe⌣it⌣is very
  pleasant.

Ernest told me⌣
  about⌣it.

I expected you⌣earlier.

I'll see you⌣out.

Ever notice that?

I⌣agree.

It's⌣all right.

I will do⌣it.

Out! Get⌣out!

All right⌣Anna.

Everything⌣all right?

Andrew did that?

Are you happy with
  Walter?

Oust the roustabouts.

Is she coming to the
  party?

Is⌣it from⌣Italy?

Oh, yes, Russell⌣is
  here.

I'll be there⌣at⌣
  eleven.

I think⌣it was
  monstrous.

I'm going to do my
  best.

Alma⌣is my name.

I can't⌣imagine⌣it.

Are you really going?

It's completely bedlam.

Is Charlotte⌣in?

I suppose so.

Imagine that!

Is the play⌣over?

It doesn't matter⌣
  anyhow.

I'll find⌣out.

Eve⌣is⌣enchanted.

It's not difficult.

Isn't that better?

Of course⌣it⌣is.

Ophelia⌣is⌣an⌣old⌣
  owl.

Icabob⌣is⌣an⌣insect.

I‿am‿Alice. I‿am‿
  eight.
It‿is‿indeed‿an‿
  old‿ogre.
Ellen‿is‿always‿
  active‿and‿always‿
  up‿in‿the‿air‿
  and‿all.
Amy‿is‿amiable‿in‿
  appearance.
Eleven‿excellent‿
  elephants‿exhibited
  ‿exaggerated‿
  external‿ears.
Oboes‿are‿instruments
  ‿in‿orchestras.

Oysters‿and‿octopi‿
  oozed‿out‿of‿
  oceans.
It‿abounds‿in‿
  excitement.
Addie‿Aurer‿is‿in‿
  Arizona.
Anna's‿umbrella‿is‿
  orange‿all‿above‿
  and‿orange‿all‿
  around‿and‿orange
  all‿over.
Edson‿is‿an‿
  honorable‿envoy.
Eva's‿expressive‿eyes
  ‿observed‿all.

To conserve the voice, as we have said you should blend words into initial vowels. If the initial vowel begins a new thought, or a breath is taken, or a pause for greater emphasis, remember—begin easily on that vowel. Watch pitch and abdominal breathing.

All‿our‿array‿is‿
  ancient.
Aunt‿Ellen‿is‿in‿
  Ohio.
Add‿all‿accounts.
It‿is‿only‿eleven‿
  o'clock.
Eddie‿is‿outdoors.

Arnold‿is‿at‿Irene's.
It‿is‿an‿obsolete‿
  item.
Ethan‿is‿always‿
  outdoors.
It‿attains‿an‿end‿
  in‿itself.

I‿urge‿all‿on‿in‿
    eager‿endeavors.

It‿is‿emphasized‿
    in‿earnest.

Oliver‿eats‿oranges‿
    every‿afternoon.

Is‿Amy‿interested‿
    in‿Atlantis?

Olsen‿is‿an‿acme‿
    of‿accomplishments.

An‿air‿brush‿is‿
    excellent.

Iceland‿oozes‿ice‿
    and‿icebergs.

Try reading this poem with easy initiation. Blend at the blending marks. If you take a breath at any of these marks, remember to initiate tone gently again.

From Song of Myself by Walt Whitman

I celebrate myself,‿and sing myself,
And what‿I‿assume you shall‿assume,
For‿every‿atom belonging to me‿as good belongs
        to you.

I loafe‿and‿invite my soul,
I lean‿and loafe‿at my‿ease
‿observing‿a spear‿
        of summer grass.

. . .

I hear bravuras‿of birds, bustle‿of growing wheat,
        gossip‿of flames, clack‿of sticks, cooking
        my meals,
I hear the sound‿I love, the sound‿of the human
        voice.

Chapter VIII

More Breathing Exercises

You now have your right pitch and are used to initiating tone easily. You are ready, then, for a few more exercises in correct breathing.

Take a breath at each diagonal mark. Remember to expand the abdominal area as you breathe in, pull in the abdomen slowly and easily as you breathe out, and say each phrase on the breath going out. Also, check your pitch frequently and watch your vowels by beginning gently at the beginning of a breath and blending in the middle.

"To a Fish," by James Henry Leigh Hunt

/ You strange, / astonished-looking, angel-faced,
/ Dreary-mouthed, gaping wretches of the sea,
/ Gulping salt water everlastingly,
/ Cold-blooded, / though with red your blood be
       graced,
/ And mute, though dwellers in the roaring waste;
/ And you, all shapes beside, that fishy be,—
/ Some round, / some flat, some long, / all devilry,
/ Legless, unloving, infamously chaste:—

/ O scaly, slippery, wet, swift, staring wights,
/ What is't ye do? / What life lead? eh, dull goggles?
/ How do ye vary your vile days and nights?
/ How pass your Sundays? / Are ye still but joggles
   In ceaseless wash? / Still nought but gapes, / and
      bites,
And drinks, and stares, / diversified with boggles?

"A Fish Answers," by James Henry Leigh Hunt

/ Amazing monster! / that, for aught I know,
/ With the first sight of thee / didst make our race
   For ever stare! / O flat and shocking face,
/ Grimly divided from the breast below!
/ Thou that on dry land horribly dost go
/ With a split body / and most ridiculous pace,
/ Prong after prong, / disgracer of all grace,
/ Long-useless-finned, haired, upright, unwet, slow!

/ O breather of unbreathable, sword-sharp air,
/ How canst exist? / How bear thyself, thou dry
   And dreary sloth? / What particle canst share
   Of the only blessed life, / the watery?
/ I sometimes see of ye an actual *pair*
   Go by! / linked fin by fin! most odiously.

From "Crossing Brooklyn Ferry," by Walt Whitman

/Flow on, river! / flow with the flood-tide, / and ebb
     with the ebb-tide!
/ Frolic on, crested and scalloped-edg'd waves!
/ Gorgeous clouds of the sunset! / drench with your
        splendour me, / or the men and women
        generations after me!

/ Cross from shore to shore, / countless crowds of passengers!

/ Stand up, / tall masts of Manhattan! / stand up, / beautiful hills of Brooklyn!

/ Throb, baffled and curious brain! / throw out questions and answers!

/ Suspend here and everywhere, / eternal float of solution!

/ Gaze, loving and thirsting eyes, / in the house or street of public assembly!

/ Sound out, voices of young men! / loudly and musically call me by my nighest name!

/ Live, old life! / play the part that looks back on the actor or actress!

/ Play the role, / the role that is great or small according as one makes it!

/ Consider, you who pursue me, / whether I may not in unknown ways be looking upon you;

/ Be firm, rail over the river, / to support those who lean idly, / yet haste with its hasting current;

/ Fly on, sea-birds! / fly sideways, / or wheel in large circles high in the air;

/ Receive the summer sky, you water, / and faithfully hold it / till all the downcast eyes have time to take it from you!

/ Diverge, fine spokes of light, / from the shape of my head, or any one's head, / in the sunlit water!

The opening section of "Calling All Stars" (Intercepted Radio Message Broadcast from the Planet Cybernetica). From *The Voice of the Dolphins and Other Short Stories,* Leo Szilard, New York, Simon and Shuster, 1961.

/ CALLING ALL STARS. / Calling all stars. / If there are any minds in the universe / capable of receiving this message, / please respond. / This is Cybernetica speaking. / This is the first message broadcast to the universe in all directions. / Normally our society is self-contained, / but an emergency has arisen and we are in need of counsel and advice.

/ Our society consists of one hundred minds. / Each one is housed in a steel casing / containing a thousand billion electrical circuits. / We think. / We think about problems which we perceive / by means of our antennae directed toward the North Star. / The solutions of these problems / we reflect back toward the North Star by means of our directed antennae. / Why we do this we do not know. / We are following an inner urge which is innate in us. / But this is only a minor one of our activities. / Mostly we think about problems which we generate ourselves. / The solutions of these problems we communicate to each other on wave length 22359.

Chapter IX

How to Get Greater Resonance

Resonance is obtained by amplifying the sound by means of the cavities of the nose, pharynx, and sinuses. The tone produced by the vocal cords alone is a thin, barely audible squeak. Resonance is really the addition of some—not too much—nasality to a voice. Therefore, the exercising of the nasal sounds "ng," "m," and "n" gives the voice more resonance. Gaining this resonance gives what we call vibrato, which is an extremely slight waver of pitch. This results in a pleasant tone with more body and fullness. Thus your voice will be full of beautiful overtones. Without these it would be colorless, hard, the tone dull and flat.

Take a new breath for each word. Remember, breathe in by expanding your abdominal area and say the word gently on the outgoing breath as you pull your abdomen in slowly and gently.

Sing each word in your optimum pitch. Hold on to the endings in a humming manner. Sustain the endings softly and gently.

For example, let's take the word "game." Sing "game" at your optimum pitch and then hold on to the final "m" in a humming fashion. Sustain the "m" for four or five seconds if it feels easy. Do not hum it too long, for then you get to that part of the air which should not be used for phonation, and which has to be forced out. If you can't sustain the "m" as long as indicated, make it shorter until you can.

The humming must be done with ease and proper breathing, never loud. This must be done at your right pitch. Tune up occasionally with your pitch pipe or at the piano, and do a few relaxing exercises in between. Don't ever do them more than five minutes at a time.

sing	jang	thing	longing
long	king	sprang	winging
fling	bong	lung	springing
wing	tongue	sprung	bringing
swing	tong	cling	hanging
rang	ping	clang	banging
song	sung	clung	slinging
ring	throng	chang	stinging
rung	pong	stung	clinging
spring	gang	string	belonging
bring	strong	along	stringing
ming	young	belong	clanging
among	hung	stung	dreaming
hang	wrong	kang	humming
bang	harangue	singing	gleaming
ting	slang	ringing	streaming
bing	sling	swinging	beaming
ling	sting	flinging	thumbing

claiming	fuming	chaining	pinning
turning	seeming	spanning	lining
steaming	sunning	spinning	gangling
coming	cunning	spooning	gonging
running	stunning	thinning	bonging
booming	staining	cleaning	pinging
blaming	laming	gleaming	janging
blooming	leaning	gloaming	thronging
teaming	loaning	summing	stringing
foaming	shunning	waning	dinging
winning	shining	panning	donging
bombing	chiming	pining	beaming

Also, for the maintenance of optimum pitch and improvement of quality, particularly resonance, sing one word to a breath, and sustain final "n" sounds at optimum pitch.

in	gone	Bonn	don
win	nine	worn	een
mean	run	on	glean
eon	noun	won	none
bone	green	moan	wren
bun	anon	grin	yen
ran	vin	bin	an
rune	rone	wan	wane
deign	loan	van	moon
lane	loon	ruin	jen
Jane	thine	Blain	bean
lon	awn	Jean	drown
gown	wean	down	vine
brown	yearn	drone	urn

Dunn	man	non	prune
lean	burn	vein	zone
line	dean	lawn	kin
drain	boon	morn	Flynn
dan	roan	pone	main
grown	mine	ton	drain
zone	soon	dean	pane
Milne	Joan	train	scone
nan	Lynne	shun	bairn
born	bairn	prone	dawn
than	dawn	gown	fern
John	din	cone	Milne
own	gun	plane	wen
main	noon	fain	throne
min	grain	run	torn
June	yon	blain	an
ban	groan	learn	man
rain	dune	crane	pine
men	yawn	scan	van
learn	wren	stein	fun
Jan	known	fawn	tone
Len	brin	glean	sign
Rhine	bran	turn	churn
dine	brine	when	preen
dane	brawn	wan	crown
gain	brown	strewn	gain
wen	brain	horn	clan
glen	gran	hen	blown
nan	then	pun	strain
blown	drawn	fine	Spain
lorn	Ben	tune	lean
earn	bane	chin	Seine

grin	Dane	shine	morn
stain	gun	June	shorn
span	clean	bane	win
than	swain	Dan	moon
yawn	line	din	pan
keen	Gran	gone	fan
spurn	Stan	clown	shown
wren	spin	rain	town
whine	drawn	twin	dine
known	scene	swoon	brown
dun	Ben	lane	can
own	shrine	vein	glen
mean	sown	groan	croon
pin	lorn	stone	twine
boon	dune	spine	swan
van	earn	thin	loan
tin	moan	lawn	skein
soon	pen	screen	stun
Joan	bun	brine	
burn	vine	none	
down	tan	scone	

Sing one word to a breath and sustain final "m" sounds at optimum pitch.

aim	limb	strum	team
poem	broom	chrome	dome
theme	clam	Brum	ream
tame	blame	calm	jam
dime	claim	swarm	came
rim	yam	Em	loam
Sam	gnome	boom	cream
come	whelm	foam	climb

numb	I'm	slim	prime
fame	bomb	plum	spoom
charm	hum	dream	spume
swim	Tom	Siam	palm
scheme	dam	storm	farm
seam	room	elm	norm
therm	term	some	pome
comb	game	hem	thumb
scrum	trim	grime	him
arm	slam	zoom	tam
swarm	flame	fume	rhyme
am	drum	alm	some
beam	frame	psalm	chum
vim	graham	warm	lime
time	swum	Pam	brim
dim	steam	mime	slim
Rome	gem	home	slum
Jim	worm	Tim	bloom
loom	groom	ram	form
crumb	charm	seem	mam
gleam	form	chime	realm
name	ohm	lamb	stream
swam	mum	sham	firm
scream	ham	slime	prim
ream	tome	plume	flume
squirm	deem	dram	shim
scum	same	from	balm
pram	firm	gram	qualm
harm	gum	helm	Nam
seam	tram	them	

Sustain "ng" and "m" and "n" sounds at

optimum pitch. Blend final "ng" sounds into initial vowels. Take a new breath on each phrase.

winging along
babbling a
  jingle
beginning a
  bloom
dangling along
rolling a dime
naming a game
blaming John
running around
during a game
going in
running on
drumming on
burning down
grooming a
  lamb
aiming a gun
beginning a
  yawn
tingling a ring
winning a game
building a bin
riding a pony
saying a rhyme
watching it
  bloom
rumbling lion
starting a run

blowing a horn
beating a drum
booming a gong
climbing a pine
zooming a gong
buying a farm
wearing a tam
making a frame
canoeing up
  stream
taking a train
flying a plane
making a gain
blowing strong
banging a drum
going to Spain
linking a chain
beating a bone
going in town
winding lane
firing a kiln
painting a faun
growing a vine
losing a game
building a bin
feeling fine
lying down
making a crown
seeing Anne

droning a tone
going around
bringing in
running on
working a churn
murmuring a
  tune
singing a song
reciting a poem
humming a tune
swinging along
slinging a stone
playing a game
putting on
gazing upon
hanging around
during a storm
going camping
hammering on
hanging a
  broom
flinging a can
bringing in
swarming
  around
spinning a form
swimming along
coming in
thinking of Pam

shearing a lamb
seeming a loom
throwing in
looking at Jim
running on
beginning a
   yawn
being a clown
cleaning a pan
eating an orange
winning a game
building a plane
riding a pony
saying a rhyme
watching it
   bloom
picking up
   crumbs
taming a lion
going in a mine
starting a run
catching a fawn
turning around
seeing Anne
blowing a horn
beating a drum
booming a gong
collecting gems
climbing a pine
having a fun
improving a
   tone

signing a paint-
   ing
working a churn
gaining a pound
beginning an
   end
leaning on
crossing the
   Seine
having a dream
becoming slim
being warm
zooming a
   chime
weighing a gram
buying a farm
wearing a tam
making a frame
canoeing up-
   stream
being firm
building a bin
becoming a dean
taking a train
lying prone
evening gown
flying a plane
wanting to learn
feeling fine
eating a prune
fixing a drain
coming at dawn

reading A. A.
   Milne
going at noon
being born
making a gain
blowing strong
losing a pen
growing a vine
getting a shine
marrying in
   June
beginning to
   rain
winding lane
mowing a lawn
putting in a
   screen
turning on a fan
going in town
crooning a song
unwinding a
   twine
firing a kiln
beating a chain
planning a
   scheme
hanging awn-
   ings

Sing the following at optimum pitch. Sustain all "ng" sounds. Take a breath frequently to prevent straining from going too long on one breath. Blend the "ng" sound into the initial vowels.

running and punning and gunning
spinning and grinning and winning
singing and flinging and swinging
tabbing and crabbing and grabbing
cracking and clacking and tracking
gliding and sliding and hiding
raiding and blockading and masquerading
jagging and flagging and tagging
sailing and hailing and trailing
gaming and aiming and acclaiming
painting and plainting and chanting
blaring and snaring and tearing
celebrating and elating and anticipating
separating and narrating and translating
shaking and breaking and quaking
brawling and sprawling and crawling
ramming and jamming and slamming
tumbling and rumbling and stumbling
scamping and stamping and tramping
dancing and prancing and advancing
banging and clanging and ganging
arranging and interchanging and exchanging
yanking and clanking and embanking
scraping and slapping and clapping
aping and shaping and draping
dreaming and scheming and beaming

darting and carting and ramparting
splashing and plashing and dashing
smashing and crashing and mashing
pasting and contrasting and wasting
chatting and batting and acrobatting
haunting and taunting and jaunting
waving and braving and conclaving
drawing and sawing and guffawing
sleighing and hooraying and disobeying
skiing and fleeing and spreeing
speeching and screeching and outreaching
speeding and conceding and heeding
peeking and seeking and sneaking
squealing and keeling and appealing
playing and saying and draying

    Sing these, sustaining your "m" and "n"
sounds at optimum pitch. Be sure to blend the
"m" and "n" sounds into vowel of "and." Take a
good abdominal breath on each line. Do not go
more than five minutes at one time. Always relax
first by doing one of the relaxing exercises.

aim and acclaim and exclaim
gain and obtain and entertain
jam and slam and ram
scan and plan and ran
yarn and tarn and darn
miasm and plasm and chasm
fawn and prawn and pawn
beam and scream and steam
glean and keen and serene

yearn and turn and churn
hem and stem and diadem
yen and pen and wren
therm and perm and term
trim and prim and grim
slim and swim and vim
grin and spin and win
chin and din and pin
Lynne and Finn and Glynne
Jim and Tim and Kim
climb and rhyme and chime
prism and schism and chrism
foam and loam and catacomb
drone and tone and blown
pom and tom and pom-pom
tom and rhom and tom-tom
don and on and on
bloom and boom and zoom
boon and croon and bassoon

Sing each word, one word to each breath. Sustain all the "m" and "n" sounds in the middle of the words. This is a very good exercise for resonance and pitch control.

many	numerous	manning	minner
manet	non-	manny	nenna
minnow	immune	manola	neiman
nominate	mammal	manuola	minnie
mingle	manner	manila	nanny
moment	moaner	mandro	minimum
mammoth	noonan	mooney	nimble

minx	nemore	manuel	manger
november	naomi	manin	momer
minute	mamie	manero	miner
number	ninny	mallon	maumer
gnomon	mineral	molino	mannion
mammy	mingo	mennell	manor
membrane	mink	nemo	mañana
meaner	minerva	nugent	manick
numan	menial	monet	manera
mannal	nomad	nonney	malone
mannino	nemean	minor	monroe
manoi	mommy	mango	menello
manus	mummer	magnet	nemer
mandell	manie	minimal	nuñez
mambu	nadeen	menu	
molnar	manello	nominee	
memmo	mannix	nominal	

Sing the words, and prolong the "m" and "n" and vowel sounds. Take one breath for each line if this is comfortable for you. If not, take two breaths for each line.

main — nonny — moment — numan
mean — ninny — numeral — nadeen
mine — nanny — November — Maine
moan — Mamie — Minerva — midnight
moon — mommy — minimal — maiden
min — momer — memmouth — Nome
man — maumer — minute — mimer
men — norman — menial — mooner
name — Manet — menu — Marmie

nim — Monet — numerous —MacDonald
nam — manner — number — namable
numb — miner — nomad — Naomi
mam — moaner — nominee — nasion
mom — mummer — non-immune — nelumbo
mum — many — gnome — Nairobian
mime — Manie — gromon — nervine
mame — money — nemean — neuron
nan — Minnie — nominal — Nevadan
nine — minimum — mammal — newness
noun — minnow — manor — nihilism
mown — mineral — membrane —nimbus
noon — minor — mammu — Nimrod
neon — nominate — manger —niobium
none — nimble — meaner — nomism
nin — magnet — Noonan — nonillion

Sing the phrases and sustain "m" and "n"
sounds at optimum pitch. Take a breath for each
phrase. You should never go too long on one breath.

nine nouns	winnie momer	nonny miner
mamie noonan	minnie mooner	dean nugent
near nome	danny dean	many names
neon numbers	jamie maumer	win one
nine mummers	main mine	minerva moore
mean man	many mines	marmie neiman
minor minerals	nine minutes	november noon
mammal mem- brane	many moons	main magnet
number nine	nadeen manello	diana raymond
manny mimer	nine minnows	eleven lemons
	eleven nomads	norman damion

manny memmo   manila rain   nurnberg ger-
janey maloney   mama nema   many
manuel manero   manono island   nova membone
minnie nuñez   manam island   novinger mis-
jeanie molnar   magnolia mary-   souri
nimble annie   land   norden germany
bunny mallon   magdalen island   new monmouth
binny mambu   madden dam   new london
mommy   mainana island   normandy mis-
  mandell   malverne new   souri
joanie manning   york   namen belgium
jonnie mennell   mallow ireland   new lebanon
nunie manus   mineral mount   penny nolan
jenny manuola   moran indiana
ginny malino   nueva gerona

Sing this exercise to increase your resonance and maintain your pitch. Sustain the "m" and "n" sounds. There are initial vowels, so begin gently on each word. Take one breath for every word because you are sustaining, and you should never sustain many words in this manner on one breath.

aluminuming   announcing   enameling
impaneling   oncoming   remonitizing
impending   nonmigrating   encumbering
communicating   companying   amending
unaccommo-   noncompen-   ammoniating
  dating   sating   determining
incriminating   morning   implanting
anathematizing   condemning   anagramma-
imprinting   reminding   tizing

demonstrating
impounding
animating
underesti-
  mating
barnstorming
comprehending
nonconforming
comprehending
emanating
remaining
enamoring
remanding

harmonizing
consuming
summoning
undermining
imponing
amounting
incoming
anastomosing
nominating
uncompro-
  mising
imagining

nonmagnet-
  izing
dominating
complementing
monumental-
  izing
compounding
emending
confirming
encamping
consummating
enumerating

Sing these lines and sustain "m" and "n" and "ng" sounds. Take many frequent breaths to avoid the strain of going too long on one breath. Keep at your optimum pitch. Be sure to blend into the vowels if it is not the beginning of a new breath. Observe the blending marks, and if you happen to take a breath on one of these marks, initiate the new tone gently.

Zinding was lingering longer‿in‿England.
The young gang swung‿along, shuffling‿and shouting.
The bilingual singer‿astonished her distinguished congregation with‿a string‿of diphthongs.
Young King Kong longed to bang‿a gong.
The songster sang‿a simple‿Armenian song.
Ming‿and Mong were sitting‿around, singing lilting songs.

Fringes of penguins hung on hangars looking like fungus.

The angry orangutan sprang to the dangling trapeze.

Sing along, sing along, sing a merry, merry song.

Jim Young, the fishmonger, sang while selling fish.

The Hong Kong longshoremen were swinging along and singing songs.

The strong gang thronged around Wingdale, Long Island.

The angler was throwing out the anchor to begin fishing for kingfish.

Sanders was yearning to conquer the Sumerian language.

It is something thumping along the banks.

Tongues are twanging and talking and clucking.

The hungry lamb began eating as he pranced in the green grass.

Darling Charline was shining and beaming as she was churning the cream in the morning.

When you begin humming with "m" or "n," remember to initiate carefully and easily, as you have learned to do when beginning with a vowel. Keep at your right pitch.

Sustain "m" and vowel sounds

```
    mmmmmmmmmmayayayayay
    mmmmmmmmmmeeeee
    mmmmmmmmmmyyyyy
    mmmmmmmmmmooooo
```

mmmmmmmmmmmuuuuu
mmmmmmmmmmmahahahahah
mmmmmmmmmmmowowowowow
mmmmmmmmmmmoyoyoyoyoy
mmmmmmmmmmmererererer
mmmmmmmmmmmuhuhuhuhuh

Sustain "n" and vowel sounds

nnnnnnnnnnnayayayayay
nnnnnnnnnnneeeee
nnnnnnnnnnnighighighighigh
nnnnnnnnnnnooooo
nnnnnnnnnnnewewewewew
nnnnnnnnnnnahahahahah
nnnnnnnnnnnowowowowow
nnnnnnnnnnnoyoyoyoyoy
nnnnnnnnnnnererererer
nnnnnnnnnnnuhuhuhuhuh

Sustain "ng" and vowel sounds

ngngngngngngngngngngngayayayayay
ngngngngngngngngngngngeeeee
ngngngngngngngngngngngiiiii
ngngngngngngngngngngngooooo
ngngngngngngngngngngnguuuuu
ngngngngngngngngngngngahahahahah
ngngngngngngngngngngngowowowowow
ngngngngngngngngngngngoyoyoyoyoy
ngngngngngngngngngngngererererer
ngngngngngngngngngngnguhuhuhuhuh

Sustain "ng" and vowel sounds

ngngAngngEngngIngngOngngU
ngngahngngowngngoyngngerngnguh

Sustain "m" and vowel sounds

MmmAmmmEmmmImmmOmmmU
mmmahmmmowmmmoymmmermmmuh

Sustain "n" and vowel sounds

nnnnnnnAnnnEnnnInnnOnnnU
nnnnnnnahnnnownnnoynnnernnnuh

Chapter X

How to Make Your Voice
Melodious and Expand Its Range

The more musical and flexible your voice, the more attractive it will be. Good speech requires a variety of pitches. The exercises in this chapter will help you expand your range and impart a melodious singing quality to your speaking voice. You are now ready to add other pitches around your optimum.

Emphasis and expression are gained, without overtaxing the larynx, through melody within one's range rather than by increased volume on stressed words. In the following exercises (see Figures 4, 5, 6, 7, 8), sing up and down in pitch gently. Always start on your optimum pitch and build up. Ascend and descend pitch only when these come with complete ease. Be sure not to practice any note which does not sound clear or come easily. An octave range of eight full notes is advantageous and healthful in developing conversational speech. You can extend this further for platform speaking, acting, or singing.

Singers should not force the voice upward before they are ready for it. Your upper notes will come automatically in time if you vocalize only on the clear and easy notes. You will find that gradually one note higher from your optimum pitch may be added. Each week, you may try one note higher, and if it sounds as clear as the lower ones, and you feel no strain and hear no roughness or breathiness, add this note. Keep adding notes until you have eight full notes, or one full octave, for general use.

Remember, don't be in a hurry to extend your range. A wide extension takes a long time, perhaps four years or more for singers. Take your time, and extend your range gradually.

A very good form of practice is to purchase some records of outstanding speakers or actors. Shakespearean actors are particularly good for using melody. Listen to how they vary the pitch to gain delicate shades of expression. Listening, and listening with concentration, is good training for your ear. Then play line for line and match your voice with the corresponding melody. We don't mean that you should imitate these actors in your conversational speech. But it is excellent practice in gaining greater flexibility in voice.

Practice inflections in pitch. These are slides from one note to another. See Figure 9 for upward and downward and other slides for the various words given. Keep within your range. These slides may be varied in any way, according to your feelings. They should not be exaggerated, but in an easy melodic flow.

We do not slide on every word. Sometimes we go directly from one note to another. Figures 10 and 11 give examples of using melody in this way for individual words with upward and downward patterns.

To impart greater use of melody in the speaking voice, sing a line according to the musical scale within your pitch range. Then speak this line with the same melody. Use poems or songs, singing one line within your range, then speaking it with the same melody. For instance, sing the Mad Hatter's song to the tune of the song Twinkle, Twinkle, Little Star, see Figure 12, and then speak it with the same melody.

Figures 13, 14, and 15 are examples of using melody in sentences. Sing the lines first, then speak them with the same melody. Make special effort to keep the last word from going below your lowest pitch or range. Since American melody pattern is a downward one predominantly at the ends of thoughts, this must be watched. To avoid this, go up at the beginning of the last word, or the second or third before the last word, and then come down. These melody patterns are given only as examples. Practice them to gain the feeling of melody. Then make your own patterns, so that you speak in your own style.

Figures 16, 17, and 18 expand these melody patterns into longer selections. Following these, additional selections are given which lend themselves to melody, and you may use them for your own melody. Think of being expressive, and changes of pitch will occur. Your voice will not only sound better, but your vocal cords will feel the difference. People who suffer from vocal fatigue know that when they speak monotonously, the fatigue increases, but when they use increased pitch changes, the fatigue disappears.

All of these are given as examples to show you how to use melody, develop greater range and flexibility.

You can also do additional selections of your own and make up your own melodies, but be sure you speak them naturally.

FIGURE 4. SING

This should be done on one breath. Start on your optimum pitch and build up. Sing the word "sing" at your optimum pitch, then sustain the "ng" in this melody pattern on the one breath. Do not go up and down on the vowel, but on the "ng." You will gain a much more beautiful, resonant voice by doing it this way. You may use all the words ending with "m" or "n" or "ng" from the previous chapters.

The first word, "sing," should be sung at

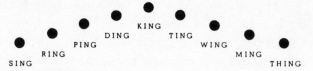

FIGURE 5.

optimum pitch with a sustaining of the "ng" sound on the same breath. Take a new breath on each word thereafter and go up in pitch one note at a time. Don't force the upper pitches. Just do them as they come in easily. Sustain the "ng" sound on each word. This exercise will give you increased resonance and melody and will expand your range.

Sing the word "sing" at optimum pitch, and sustain the "ng" on one breath. As you come down,

FIGURE 6.

add "a song" on the same breath. Do this also with the other "ng" phrases on previous pages. For instance:

booming a gong
climbing a pine
zooming a gong
buying a farm
wearing a tam
making a frame
taking a train
droning a tone
flying a plane
making a gain
shearing a lamb
seeming a loom
being a clown
winning a game

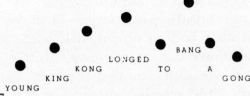

FIGURE 7.

Sing "young" at optimum pitch and sustain the "ng." Go up in pitch for the other notes, always sustaining the "ng" sound. Breathe when necessary.

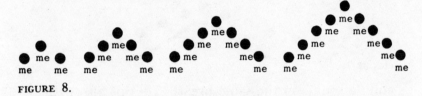

FIGURE 8.

Continue in the same way on the following syllables and words:

may	neigh	main	neam	mam
my	knee	mean	nam	mom
mo	no	mine	name	mame
moo	new	moan	nim	nine
mah	now	moon	numb	none
moy	ner	min	nown	noon
mow	nah	man	men	mown
mer	noy	mime	mon	nin

Start each word at your optimum pitch and add notes going up. Never strain to get a higher note, just do them as you can do them with ease. Breathe whenever necessary. Again we remind you, never exercise more than five minutes at a time.

This is where we transfer the singing type of exercises to natural speaking.

Speak each word on one breath. The lowest tone should always be your optimum pitch. For instance, say "how" at optimum pitch and slide up. Go down the whole column in this manner, sliding up on each word and starting each at your optimum pitch.

In the second column beginning with "airy," you should start two or three notes above your optimum pitch and slide down to your optimum.

In the third column, begin "authenticate" at optimum pitch, slide up and back down again.

In the next column, start a couple of notes above optimum and slide down and then up. The greater the variation in pitch, the greater the expression. But guard against sounding affected by using too much variation on one word.

FIGURE 9.

/	\	⌒
how	airy	authen-
up-	edge	ticate
fife	sphere	revolving
more	clouds	centripetal
wood	move	acrimo-
such	wings	nious
rain	change	polemics
glass	please	Louisiana
first	wind	unhealthy
will	birds	reaction
have	when	specific

flame
part
way
round
right
and
the
we
share
of
shore

much
helm
straight
slant
down
fly
guide
work
space
paint
make

Leonardo
untram-
 meled
continuous
collection
distribu-
 tion
photogra-
 phy
adventi-
 tious
American
deliberate
implica-
 tions
remaining
pleasure
transition

attitude
antiquated
probably
theory
c̀ylinder
overture
literary
interests
purposes
floating
dignified

boundary
northwest-
 ern
bedeviled
impetus
conse-
 quently
occupying
separating
following
finishing

casual
treatment
function-
  ing
person
organisms
dandelions
warning
adjective
atlas
prejudice
common

counter-
  poise
gravity
rectangles
uniformity
afterwards
exigencies
shovelful
combatant
density
atmosphere
Delano
opposite
pyramid

These exercises are the same, but they go from note to note instead of sliding up and down. Say the first part of "Philip" at optimum pitch, say the second syllable at a higher pitch, and so forth. The lowest pitch should always be your optimum pitch. For instance, start "Harriet" a note or two above optimum and come down to optimum on the second syllable.

Speak all these words naturally. If you find difficulty in speaking them at your notes, sing the word first and then speak it afterward. The only real difference between speaking and singing is that in singing you sustain the notes, and in speaking you go more quickly from note to note without sustaining.

FIGURE 10.

Philip	eleven	Harriet
swinging	galloping	hurriedly
between	buffaloes	photographed
seven	rollicking	chattering
hammocks	liltingly	Eleanor
whizzing	oftentimes	scampering
whirling	silently	Frederick
spinning	frequently	skeltering
rolling	savagely	Agatha
tumbling	breezily	scurrying
wriggling	hovering	Theodore
wincing	easily	fidgety
scuffling	approaching	Francisca
clinging	thunderous	muttering
jumping	cavorting	Margaret
bounding	suddenly	pummeling
thrashing	corralling	Pamela
clasping	larruping	prattling
shouting	lazily	Priscilla
singing	portraying	finally
laughing	radiant	completely
hooting	quietude	exhausted

illuminate	beautifully	anthropology
illustrious	operatic	supercilious
intelligent	promenading	archipelago
meridian	Katherina	superficially

constructional
ability
progressively
intensively
apparently
peculiarly

spontaneous
preferably
generally
necessary
literary
economic

dermatologist
equanimity
etymology
aborigines
surreptitiously
alimentary

FIGURE 11.

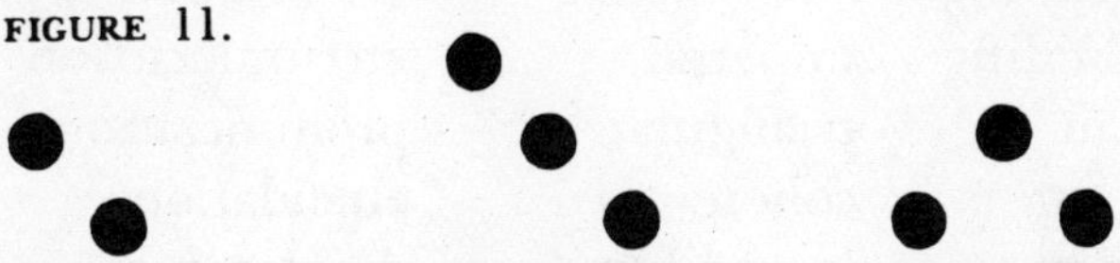

early
morning
shadows
moving
sprightly
fiery
tempests
blowing
fiercely
endless
glowworms
shining
in the
duskness
Homer
hammers
gaily
whistling
making
tables
by the
dozen

antelopes
buffalo
baritone
suddenly
twistery
trippingly
twittering
tentative
radiate
Joliet
astronaut
tubular
evident
mocking bird
devil fish
wandering
wondering
anchoring
katydid
government
rectangle
musical

fantastic
reciting
abounding
astonished
perplexing
surprising
decadence
reporter
forgotten
enhearten
enchanted
triumphant
important
disputant
consistent
secluded
attended
delightful
Jamaica
acumen
unlikely
September

● ●   ●   ●
   ● ●   ●   ●   ●   ● ●   ● ●

manufacture	incorporate	agglomeration
presentation	explosively	alliteration
demonstrating	magnificent	articulation
understanding	imperial	circumlocution
European	triangular	pronunciation
circulation	coherently	elucidation
respiration	incredibly	desideratum
evidently	orangutan	edification
introducing	especially	emancipation
giant panda	acclimatize	enunciation

THE MAD HATTER'S SONG   by Lewis Carroll

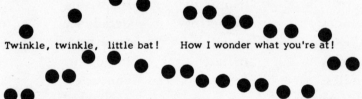

Twinkle, twinkle, little bat!   How I wonder what you're at!

Up above the world you fly, Like a tea-tray in the sky. Twinkle, twinkle-

FIGURE 12.

From the *Collected Verse of Lewis Carroll* by Charles L. Dodgson, used with permission of The Macmillan Company.

Start at óptimum pitch and go higher when the dots go up. Take a breath when necessary.

FIGURE 13.

Just now?	Just now.	Right now?	Right now!
They are?	I've heard.	You would?	Now! Now!
Ready?	Go on.	See now?	I see.
Hello Lee.	Hello, Kirk.	Come here!	Right away.
		Look out!	Oh, yes!
Oscar?	Yes, dear.	All right?	All right
Finished?	Not yet.	Why not?	You'll see.
Did you?	I will.	Wasn't it?	It wasn't.
What time?	Seven o'clock.	Did he?	He did.
Think so?	Yes, sir.	Did you?	That's right.
Of what?	Water power.	See it?	I do.
Can't you?	Of course.	Good afternoon!	Good afternoon.
Harry! Harry!	Be still.	Jim! Jim!	Right here.
How soon?	Right away.	Remember Alice?	I remember.
What's that?	You heard.	What happened?	Stop shouting.
Take it.	O. K.		Stop
So long.	Good-bye.	Why? Why?	screaming.
Good morning!	Good day!	What? What?	Talk quietly.
Good evening!	Good evening!		Don't worry.
Hello!	Hello!	Sounds bad. Think so?	I'm sure.

FIGURE 14.

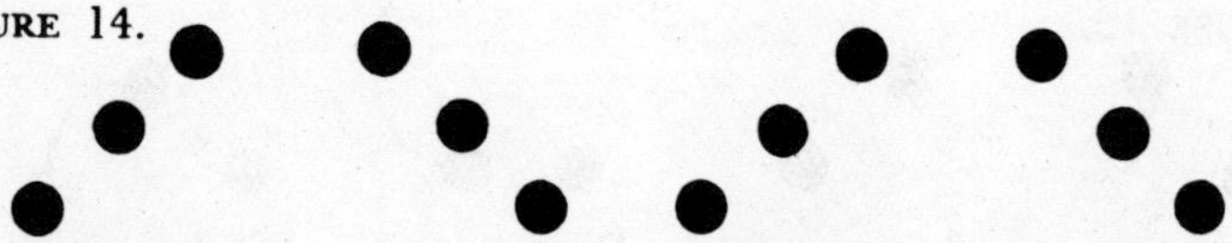

How are
you?

What is it?

Where are
you?

Where is
Joe?

How was it?

Are you
hungry?

Is this
right?

Did you
call?

Who is
Henry?

How is
Helen?

Is dinner
ready?

How are
you?

Have some
milk?

Where's
your
mother?

Can't you
tell?

I feel fine.

The bell's
ringing.

I'm out
here.

Joe is out.

It was great.

No, I'm
not.

Yes, it is.

Yes, at
nine.

Henry
Adams.

Helen's all
right.

In five min-
utes.

Fine, thank
you.

No, thank
you.

In Okla-
homa.

Not today.

What's
your
name?

Have you
noticed?

Is he eager?

What was
it?

Didn't you
know?

Were you
whistling?

Can you
whistle?

Teach me
how?

Did she go?

To Chi-
cago?

May I
really?

What is
true?

Really,
Leo?

You aren't
playing?

John
McGrew.

I should
say.

Very, very
eager.

I don't
know.

Yes, I
knew.

I was
whistling.

Anybody
can
whistle.

Just like
this.

An hour
ago.

I suppose
so.

Better ask
Mama.

That's the
question.

Really,
Regina.

Not today.

Are you working?	No, not yet.	Is he boring?	Of course not.
Going out?	In a minute.	Will you stay?	For a while.
		Remember Ben?	Certainly.

Start "How are you?" at optimum pitch and go up. Start "I feel fine" a few notes above optimum and come down. It's easier to do the question immediately followed by the answer. "How are you?" Then, "I feel fine." Take breaths whenever necessary and be careful with your vowels.

FIGURE 15.

Where is Helen?	She's in the kitchen.
What are you doing?	Looking for the key.
Where have you been?	I've been to the movies.
Didn't you hear me?	No, I didn't hear you.
Are the boys in?	Yes, they are sleeping.
Is there any cheese?	I'll make a sandwich.
Do you like grapes?	Of course, I like grapes.
What do you want?	I'd like a hamburger.
Did you mention Fred?	Yes, he's in Idaho.
Did he leave home?	Oh, it was months ago.
How is everyone?	They are all fine.
How did you know?	Johnny told me yesterday.
What are you doing?	I'm reading a good book.
May we play out?	No, you may not now.
Did you hear it?	No, I never heard it.
What did he say?	He said he liked you.
Where is Allen?	He's away a great deal.

Was it exciting?	Yes, it was very exciting.
What did you expect?	Well, I don't really know.
May I help you?	I'd like some water.
Did you dream it?	No, it was no dream.
What's this all about?	Well, now I'll tell you.

FIGURE 16.

I will sing! O, I will walk from a glen to a fall,

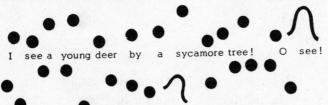

Full of music and song, I will sing and wander up and cross the river !

I see a young deer by a sycamore tree! O see!

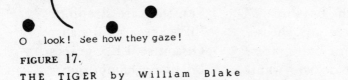

And another one! Watch as they turn together like twins!

O look! See how they gaze!

FIGURE 17.

THE TIGER by William Blake

Tiger! Tiger! burning bright In the forests of the night, What

immortal hand or eye Could frame thy fearful symmetry?

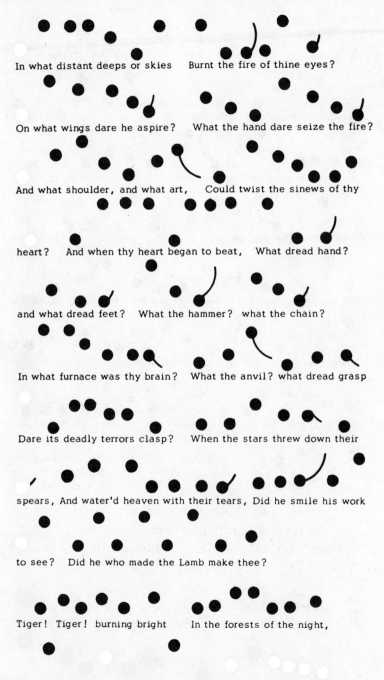

In what distant deeps or skies   Burnt the fire of thine eyes?

On what wings dare he aspire?   What the hand dare seize the fire?

And what shoulder, and what art,   Could twist the sinews of thy

heart?   And when thy heart began to beat,   What dread hand?

and what dread feet?   What the hammer? what the chain?

In what furnace was thy brain?   What the anvil? what dread grasp

Dare its deadly terrors clasp?   When the stars threw down their

spears, And water'd heaven with their tears, Did he smile his work

to see?   Did he who made the Lamb make thee?

Tiger! Tiger! burning bright   In the forests of the night,

What immortal hand or eye, Dare frame thy fearful symmetry?

FIGURE 18.

A cutting from CANDIDA by George Bernard Shaw

Candida: Are you going, Eugene? Well, dear me, just look at you,

going out in the street in that state! You are a poet, certainly.

Look at him, James! Look at his collar! Look at his tie! look at

his hair! One would think someone had been throttling you. Here!

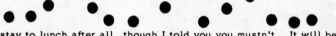

Stand still. There! Now you look so nice that I think you'd better

stay to lunch after all, though I told you you mustn't. It will be

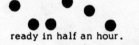

ready in half an hour.

Used by permission of:
The Society of Authors
of The United Kingdom.

Make up your own melody pattern. Bring out the feeling through melody.

From Act III, Scene II, *Hamlet,* by William Shakespeare.

HAMLET: Speak the speech, I pray you, as I pronounced it to you, trippingly on the tongue: but if you mouth it, as many of your players do, I had as lief the town-crier spoke my lines. Nor do not saw the air too much with your hand, thus; but use all gently: for in the very torrent, tempest, and, as I may say, whirlwind of passion, you must acquire and beget a temperance that may give it smoothness. O, it offends me to the soul to hear a robustious periwig-pated fellow tear a passion to tatters, to very rags, to split the ears of the groundlings, who, for the most part, are capable of nothing but inexplicable dumb-shows and noise; I would have such a fellow whipped for o'erdoing Termagant; it out-herods Herod: pray you, avoid it.

Be not too tame neither, but let your own discretion be your tutor. Suit the action to the word, the word to the action. . . . Go, make you ready.

Speak the following scene with your own melody patterns. This is from *Blithe Spirit* by Noel Coward.

RUTH: When did you first discover that you had these extraordinary powers?
MADAME ARCATI: When I was quite tiny. My mother was a medium before me, you know, so I had every opportunity of starting on the ground floor as you might say. I had my first trance when I was four years old and my first protoplasmic manifestation when I was five and a half—what an exciting day that was, I

shall never forget it—of course the manifestation itself was quite small and of very short duration, but, for a child of my tender years, it was most gratifying.

From *Blithe Spirit,* by Noel Coward, copyright 1941 by Noel Coward, reprinted by permission of Doubleday & Co., Inc.

Chapter XI

How to Get Volume with Ease

After you have practiced the exercises in the preceding chapters for a month to six weeks, you should be speaking or singing consistently without vocal fatigue. When you feel satisfied that you are doing this, you are ready for greater volume. You have now learned to expel your breath easily and slowly as you speak in normal volume. Now, when you want to increase this volume, you will expel the air at a faster rate. But this should be done by pulling in the abdominal muscles, *not* by tightening the muscles of the larynx.

As you close a bellows slowly, the air comes out slowly. As you close a bellows quickly, the air comes out more quickly. This is also true in breathing. The best way to control the rate of air and make it come out more quickly is to tense or contract the abdominal muscles. Think of pulling in your stomach or pushing it in with a book if necessary. Feel the expansion around the waist area as you breathe in, and then press in quickly to make the air come out more quickly, and automatically you will have more volume.

On the whole, a loud voice is unpleasant, but there are times when we need volume. So practice volume for use when you need it and when it is appropriate, as in a crowded room, in a restaurant, or at a distance.

To repeat, the proper way to let air out faster is by abdominal action control. Try first with breath alone. Stand up, for it is easier to gain volume correctly standing erect. Good posture is necessary for good voice, and it is of prime importance for volume increase. If you are in a position which cramps the abdominal area, you cannot control it. Take a deep breath through the nose. Expand your stomach. Don't take as much air as possible, for this, too, causes excessive tension. But take a relatively deep breath so that there is nice expansion of the abdominal muscles. Then pull in the abdominal muscles quickly and let the air flow out with breath alone. You should feel no strain in your throat. If you do, you are not ready for volume, so wait a week or more until you can do it with ease. Then do the same on the following words beginning with "h" (see list). Breathe first, then say each word as you pull your stomach in. You may increase the volume in steps rather than trying for lots of volume immediately like this.

howl   HowL   HOWL

1. Do a few relaxing exercises first.
2. Do the first word on your optimum pitch and let the pitch go up a little for louder words, but not too high.

3. Breathe in by expanding the stomach area. Take a new breath for each word.
4. Say each word as you expel the air from the stomach area by pulling your stomach in.

Do the words beginning with consonants first, and then when you become used to these, do the ones beginning with vowels.

bang	BANG	hurry	HURRY
boom	BOOM	shout	SHOUT
boomlay	BOOMLAY	flash	FLASH
clang	CLANG	crash	CRASH
jang	JANG	flap	FLAP
chop	CHOP	slam	SLAM
beat	BEAT	look	LOOK
hang	HANG	snap	SNAP
hail	HAIL	help	HELP
howl	HOWL	police	POLICE
row	ROW	go	GO
sling	SLING	ram	RAM
stop	STOP	draw	DRAW
halt	HALT	cut	CUT
war	WAR	roll	ROLL
run	RUN	set	SET
speed	SPEED	hello	HELLO
faster	FASTER	blow	BLOW
spin	SPIN	shoot	SHOOT
fling	FLING	no	NO
glory	GLORY	bong	BONG
quiet	QUIET	fire	FIRE
charge	CHARGE	ready	READY

salaam	SALAAM	splash	SPLASH
gamin	GAMIN	clash	CLASH
gong	GONG	hello	HELLO
hallelu-	HALLELU-	hang	HANG
jah	JAH	bong	BONG
hoodoo	HOODOO	blow	BLOW
thunder	THUNDER	no	NO
noise	NOISE	lightning	LIGHT-
climb	CLIMB		NING
revenge	REVENGE	crush	CRUSH
murder	MURDER	yes	YES
treason	TREASON	chime	CHIME
smash	SMASH		

Don't forget to take a new breath for each word.

flare	FLARE	gunfire	GUNFIRE
crack	CRACK	shoot	SHOOT
rage	RAGE	turbu-	TURBU-
storm	STORM	lence	LENCE
violence	VIOLENCE	burst	BURST
despera-	DESPERA-	mon-	MON-
tion	TION	strous	STROUS
fury	FURY	mighty	MIGHTY
cyclone	CYCLONE	colossal	COLOSSAL
sand-	SAND-	gigantic	GIGANTIC
storm	STORM	giants	GIANTS
thunder-	THUNDER-	slap	SLAP
burst	BURST	lollop	LOLLOP
demon	DEMON	whale	WHALE
romp	ROMP	boil	BOIL
rush	RUSH	bulge	BULGE

higher	HIGHER	march	MARCH
pump	PUMP	mount	MOUNT
wildfire	WILDFIRE	dis-	DIS-
huff	HUFF	mount	MOUNT
puff	PUFF	roar	ROAR
strangle	STRANGLE	load	LOAD
faraway	FARAWAY	cast	CAST
far off	FAR OFF	ram	RAM
beam	BEAM	ready	READY
sky high	SKY HIGH	set	SET
sound	SOUND	attention	ATTEN-
sink	SINK		TION
pull	PULL	saddle	SADDLE
drag	DRAG	signal	SIGNAL
force	FORCE	present	PRESENT
power	POWER	carry	CARRY
break up	BREAK UP	draw	DRAW
waste	WASTE	sabers	SABERS
crack	CRACK	return	RETURN
collapse	COLLAPSE	guard	GUARD
devasta-	DEVASTA-	point	POINT
tion	TION	front	FRONT
shatter	SHATTER	rear	REAR
tear	TEAR	cut	CUT
break	BREAK	shoot	SHOOT
pluck	PLUCK	parry	PARRY
squelch	SQUELCH	bombs	BOMBS
gut	GUT	load	LOAD
ravage	RAVAGE	vault	VAULT
devour	DEVOUR	pack	PACK
wail	WAIL	roll	ROLL
stand	STAND	block	BLOCK

collide	COLLIDE	ram	RAM
fight	FIGHT	shove	SHOVE
crack	CRACK	push	PUSH
cannons	CANNONS	hustle	HUSTLE
whack	WHACK	wallop	WALLOP
thwack	THWACK	douse	DOUSE
bump	BUMP	throw	THROW
knock	KNOCK	strike	STRIKE
stroke	STROKE	blast	BLAST
punch	PUNCH	whip	WHIP
swat	SWAT	run	RUN
sweep	SWEEP	fly	FLY
thump	THUMP	bolt	BOLT
thrust	THRUST	dart	DART
pass	PASS	bound	BOUND
jab	JAB	spring	SPRING
rap	RAP	sizzle	SIZZLE
clip	CLIP	hop	HOP
swing	SWING	gallop	GALLOP
spank	SPANK	trot	TROT
chop	CHOP	canter	CANTER
kick	KICK	spur	SPUR
hammer	HAMMER	hasten	HASTEN

Be extremely careful when you begin the following initial vowel words. Initiate gently, so that you don't bang too hard. Since the air is coming out faster, you are naturally using the air faster, and necessarily you must take even more frequent breaths to avoid strain. Pushing in on the abdomen to let the air out fast is like pushing in on the gas pedal to make the car go faster, giving it more gas.

At first, push the waist area in with your hands if the muscles aren't yet strong enough to do the work on their own. These muscles must be strengthened to become accustomed to controlling the rate at which the air escapes. For a really loud yell, you will use all the air you can without strain on one word. So it is impossible to yell very loudly very long on one breath without straining. Some use more volume than necessary. You must learn to use only the amount of volume necessary under given circumstances. In speaking before a large audience, always insist on an amplification system. You still need more volume with an amplifier than in conversation in a quiet room, but not nearly so much as without the microphone in speaking before larger audiences.

These are to be done in the same manner as the preceding words, but are designed especially for practice in easy initiation on the vowels. Extra attention must be given so as not to bang the vocal cords too hard. "H" words are used first. In the beginning both words begin with "h." The first word (those in lower case) is spoken softly, then you should take another breath and say the second word (those in upper case) louder. Then when you come to those exercises with one word beginning with "h" and the one next to it beginning with a vowel, say both loud, with a new breath on each and paying particular attention to the second. Be sure you begin this second word starting with the vowel with ease and gently, even though you are saying it loudly.

You must remember to take a new breath on each word. Breathe in through your mouth, expanding the abdominal area, then say each word as you quickly pull in your abdomen. You get your power from this quick pulling in of the abdominal area.

If you should still have some difficulty, begin the vowels softly and then swell in volume. Practice this way until you can begin with ease in a loud tone.

Keep on optimum pitch or a little above.

WORD LIST FOR PROJECTION

hail	HAIL	Harley	HARLEY
heel	HEEL	hasten	HASTEN
howl	HOWL	haul	HAUL
hello	HELLO	ha	HA
hurray	HURRAY	haw	HAW
hurrah	HURRAH	hi	HI
help	HELP	ho	HO
hang	HANG	Hazel	HAZEL
halt	HALT	hear	HEAR
hurry	HURRY	bang	BANG
Harry	HARRY		
Hannah	HANNAH	HAY	AYE
hallelu-	HALLE-	HUP	UP
jah	LUJAH	HIGH	I
Hilda	HILDA	HO	OH
Holly	HOLLY	HE	EE
hark	HARK	HOW	OW
harken	HARKEN	HARVEY	ARVEY

HAWAY	AWAY	HAMY	AMY
HALARM	ALARM	HANNAH	ANNA
HEXTRA	EXTRA	HAN	ANN
HAHOY	AHOY	HARSON	ARSON
HALL	ALL	HEARTY	ARTIE
HESTER	ESTHER	HASSAS-	ASSASSIN
HABOVE	ABOVE	SIN	
HELEN	ELLEN	HUMP	UMPH
HARRY	'ARRY	HOONA	OONA
HIKE	IKE	HAUDA-	AUDA-
HALLAH	ALLAH	CIOUS	CIOUS
HAIM	AIM	HUPHILL	UPHILL
HAMEN	AMEN	HUP-	UPHOLD
HABIT	ABBOT	HOLD	
HABOUT	ABOUT	HOBEY	OBEY
HOMAR	OMAR	HOBJEC-	OBJEC-
HOUT	OUT	TION	TION
HA-	AROUND	HUP-	UPSTAGE
ROUND		STAGE	
HADA	ADA	HAVENGE	AVENGE
HIDA	IDA	HUP-	UP-
HACTION	ACTION	STAIRS	STAIRS
HAHA	AHA	HOVER	OVER
HOHO	OHO	HORDER	ORDER
HALEX	ALEX	HOPEN	OPEN
HALBERT	ALBERT	HELLIS	ELLIS
HALLEY	ALI	HETHAN	ETHAN
HALINE	ALINE	HEDITH	EDITH
HALISON	ALLISON	HETHEL	ETHEL
HALLEN	ALLEN	HEAVE	EVE
HALL-	ALWAYS	HIS	IS
WAYS		HINEZ	INEZ

Do the words in lower case softly and in upper case louder. For instance, able (soft) then ABLE (loud). There should be easy initiation on all.

able	ABLE
Amy	AMY
Edmund	EDMUND
Oliver	OLIVER
Esther	ESTHER
I	I
Ingrid	INGRID
Uncle	UNCLE
Aunt	AUNT
arm	ARM
undo	UNDO
up	UP
on	ON
oh	OH
above	ABOVE
Eddie	EDDIE
Ellen	ELLEN
Andrew	ANDREW
Abe	ABE
Ava	AVA
Ida	IDA
Erma	ERMA
Ike	IKE
over	OVER
off	OFF
abroad	ABROAD

More air supply is needed for saying more words on a breath. When you increase volume the

air comes out faster and is used up more quickly.
So take in more air, expel it by pulling in your
stomach quickly, pushing the air out faster. Say each
phrase on one breath.

Ship ahoy

All aboard

What ho

Ho there

Allah on high

Beat a charge

Hail to the Chief

Yo ho ho

Forward march

Present arms

Order arms

Left right left right

Row vassals row

Stretch to your oars

Who goes there

Bang a gong

Beat a drum

Blow a bugle

Charge for the guns

Stop it

Ring the alarm

Quiet quiet please

Bombs away

Throw it out

Glory, glory, hallelujah

Going going going gone

Flap and bang

Crash and clash

Thunder and lightning

Stop the music

Murder and treason

Blow, bugles, blow

Hurry hurry hurry

Close in

Back up

Pick up the beat

Let her run

Man the guns

Hit the deck

Eyes right

From pole to pole

Wide and broad

Wide-winged and broad-
   tailed

Force and blast

Full steam ahead

Step up

Havoc and ruin

Shatter and crumble

Crush to atoms

Wipe out

Throw down

Swallow up

On high

Up in the air
In the clouds
Unfathomable deeps
Ocean depths
Gut with fire
Fire and sword
Fling a stone
Cut through the trees
Beat the bones
Come one, come all
Slam and bang
Ring the bell
String him up
Throw him into the
  dungeon
Hang the traitor
Ding dong ding dong
Guide right
Eyes right
Eyes left
Left half face
Left oblique march
Right oblique march
Right half face
Support arms
Sling carbine
Cast about
Let her run all
Thar she blows
Man the pumps
Strike up the band
Strike one, strike two,
  strike three, you're out

Hit the line
Go go go
Fight the fight
Man the guns
Hit the deck
Run for cover
Swim or sink
Back water starboard
Back water port
Starboard oars up
Port oars up
Back her down port
Give your all
Hup one hup two hup
  three
Pick it up starboard
Pick it up port
Lean to port
Lean to starboard
Ship oars
Charge cartridge
Fire the guns
Fire fire fire
Ram cartridge
Carry lance
Present lance
charge lances
Order lances
Draw saber
Present saber
Inspection of arms
Inspection of saber
Left moulinet

Right moulinet

Rear moulinet

In tierce, point

Left point

Right point

Rear point

Against infantry, left—
point

Front cut

Left cut

Right cut

Rear cut

In tierce—parry

For the head—parry

Against infantry right—
parry

Carry lances

Front point

Right rear, point

To the ground, point

Left rear lances

Left rear, point

To the ground, point

Shoulder arms

Right shoulder arms

Left shoulder arms

Port arms

Right face

Left face

About face

Present arms

Port arms

Order arms

Right front into line

Left front into line

To the rear march

Right wheel march

Left wheel march

Squads right and left
march

Block the line

Here comes the chopper

Ram cartridge

Eagle spread

Lightning speed

Pick up speed

Speed up

Cut and run

Pack on sail

Run a race

Act with haste

Run wide open

Step along

Carry sail

Crowd sail

Give her beans

Go all out

Go at full blast

March in double quick
time

Put on more speed

Hurry up

Crack on

Gain ground

Carry on

Break open

Burst out
Rage and storm
Fierce as a tiger
Might and main
Brute force
At the point of the
  bayonet
With a vengeance
It's outrageous
On a rampage
Tear it up
Throw it out
Romp and rush
Bear down
Kick up
Hail Columbia

Monstrous villain
You hippopotamus
Whack and bang
Bump and thump
Splash and slap
Get out
Huff and puff
Dry up
Over the hills
Out of range
At a distance
Farther away
All aboard
Far and wide
To the uttermost parts
  of the earth

Increase volume for volume practice.

One of Katharina's speeches from *The Taming of the Shrew*, Act IV, Scene III, by William Shakespeare.

KATHARINA: The more my wrong, the more
    his spite appears:
What, did he marry me to famish me?
Beggars, that come unto my father's door,
Upon entreaty have a present alms;
If not, elsewhere they meet with charity:
But I, who never knew how to entreat,
Nor never needed that I should entreat,
Am starved for meat, giddy for lack of sleep;

With oaths kept waking, and with brawling
    fed:
And that which spites me more than all these
    wants,
He does it under name of perfect love;
As who should say, if I should sleep or eat,
'Twere deadly sickness or else present death.
I prithee go, and get me some repast;
I care not what, so it be wholesome food.

Jelly Joe

Hurry! Hurry! Hurry! Step right up into the
tent behind us and see Jelly Joe, the jell-
boned boy! Every joint in his body bends like
a piece of putty. He crawls on his belly like
a snake. Come see curvy curvy Jelly Joe crawl.
Step right this way, ladies and gentlemen, for
twenty-five cents, one quarter, one-fourth of a
dollar. Hurry! Hurry! Hurry!

The Bomb Factory

This morning I visited a big bomb factory. It
was on a high hill. All around were low
valleys. I ran up to the entrance, pushed open
a sliding door, and walked down a long hall-
way. There I stepped into an elevator, pushed
the B button and went down to the basement.
As the door opened, I saw little bombs,
medium-sized bombs, and tremendous bombs.
Suddenly, the bombs started going off. The big
bombs went bang! The middle-sized bombs
went bang! And the tiny bombs went poof!
With a start, I awoke, and found it was but
a dream.

The following is a speech given by Marianne from the screenplay, *Wild Strawberries,* by Ingmar Bergman, published by Simon & Schuster. Credit JANUS Films Inc., New York.

MARIANNE: You are an old egotist, Father. You are completely inconsiderate and you have never listened to anyone but yourself. All this is well hidden behind your mask of old-fashioned charm and your friendliness. But you are hard as nails, even though everyone depicts you as a great humanitarian. We who have seen you at close range, we know what you really are. You can't fool us. For instance, do you remember when I came to you a month ago? I had some idiotic idea that you would help Evald and me. So I asked to stay with you for a few weeks. Do you remember what you said?

From Scene I of *The Frogs,* a play written in 406 B.C. by the Greek dramatist Aristophanes.

CHARON: (To Dionysus) Sit to the oar. (Calling) Who else for the boat? Be quick.
(To Dionysus) Hi! what are you doing?
DIONYSUS: What am I doing? Sitting
On to the oar. You told me to, yourself.
CHARON: Now sit you there, you little Potgut.
DIONYSUS: So?
CHARON: Now stretch your arms full length before you.
DIONYSUS: So?

CHARON: Come, don't keep fooling; plant your
feet and now Pull with a will.

DIONYSUS: Why, how am *I* to pull?
I'm not an oarsman, seaman, Salaminian.
I can't!

CHARON: You can. Just dip your oar in once.
You'll hear the loveliest timing songs.

DIONYSUS: What from?

CHARON: Frog-swans, most wonderful.

DIONYSUS: Then give the word.

CHARON: Heave ahoy! heave ahoy!

FROGS: Brekekekex, ko-ax, ko-ax,
                Brekekekex, ko-ax ko-ax!

We children of the fountain and the lake
        Let us wake
Our full choir-shout, as the flutes are ringing out,
        Our symphony of clear-voiced song.
The song we used to love in the Marshland up above,
        In praise of Dionysus to produce,
        Of Nysaean Dionysus, son of Zeus,
When the revel-tipsy throng, all crapulous and gay,
To our precinct reeled along on the holy Pitcher Day,
        Brekekekex, ko-ax, ko-ax.

DIONYSUS: O, dear O, dear! now I declare

FROGS: I've got a bump upon my rump,

DIONYSUS: Brekekekex, ko-ax, ko-ax.

FROGS: But you, perchance, don't care.

DIONYSUS: Brekekekex, ko-ax, ko-ax.
                Hang you, and your ko-axing too!

FROGS: There's nothing for ko-ax with you.
                That is right, Mr. Busybody, right!
                    For the Muses of the lyre love us
                    well;
And hornfoot Pan who plays
                    on the pipe his jocund lays;

And Apollo, Harper bright,
                    in our Chorus takes delight;
For the strong reeds sake
                    which I grow within my lake
          To be girdled in his lyre's deep shell.
                    Brekekekex, ko-ax, ko-ax.
DIONYSUS: My hands are blistered very sore;
          My stern below is sweltering so,
          'Twill soon, I know, upturn and roar
          Brekekekex, ko-ax, ko-ax.
          O tuneful race, O pray give o'er,
          O sing no more.
FROGS: Ah, no! ah, no!
          Loud and louder our chant must flow.
     ~   Sing if ever ye sang of yore,
          When in sunny and glorious days
          Through the rushes and marsh-flags
                    springing
          On we swept, in the joy of singing
          Myriad-diving roundelays.
          Or when fleeing the storm, we went
          Down to the depths, and our choral song
          Wildly raised to a loud and long
          Bubble-bursting accompaniment.
FROGS AND DIONYSUS:
          Brekekekex, ko-ax, ko-ax.
DIONYSUS: This timing song I take from you.
FROGS: That's a dreadful thing to do.
DIONYSUS: Much more dreadful, if I row
          till I burst myself, I trow.
FROGS AND DIONYSUS:
          Brekekekex, ko-ax, ko-ax.
          Go, hang yourselves; for what care I?
FROGS: All the same we'll shout and cry,
          Stretching all our throats with song,

Shouting, crying, all day long.

FROGS AND DIONYSUS:

Brekekekex, ko-ax, ko-ax.

DIONYSUS: In this you'll never, never win.

FROGS: This you shall not beat us in.

DIONYSUS: No, nor ye prevail o'er me.

Never! Never! I'll be my song

Shout, if need be, all day long.

Until I've learned to master your ko-ax.

Brekekekex, ko-ax, ko-ax.

I thought I'd put a stop to your ko-ax.

CHARON: Stop! Easy! Take the car and push
her to. Now pay your fare and go.

Chapter XII

Making the New Voice Habitual

We have now learned to exercise at the proper pitch and range and to initiate tone gently in words and sentences. Now you must begin to carry this over automatically to spontaneous speech. You will accomplish this gradually. Don't expect it to occur all at once or even the first week. But it will come.

The exercises will, of course, help the carry-over, especially if you do them frequently throughout the day in short, two to five-minute practice periods. You may even increase your practice period to fifteen minutes at a time now. The more often you do them, the more the carry-over will be effected. Immediately after a practice period, you are likely to be speaking in your new voice; but then, after a while, you may tend to slip back into your old vocal habits. The more frequently you practice during the day the quicker the carry-over. In the beginning you will be doing well to say the words properly, and then sentences, and then reading poetry and prose. Another helpful thing to do is to read aloud from plays, as this is conversational speech. And you must practice conversation itself.

Talk to yourself or talk to others while keeping in mind all the points required for your new voice. It is wise to carry a pitch pipe or pitch instrument around with you at all times and tune up as often as you can. Do this especially whenever you answer the telephone. Before answering, blow your correct pitch, say "Hello" at it before you say "Hello" on the telephone.

Sometimes a person will be hesitant emotionally about using a new voice with friends, to whom his new voice seems strange. If this is so for you, you may find it helpful to go out and talk with strangers, to go into stores and talk with sales clerks, using the new pitch in this manner until they become more accustomed to it.

Recording the voice helps to carry over the new voice to conversational speech. In the absence of a recording machine, you may stand in the corner of a room and hear your voice reverberate from the walls into your ears. Also, saying phrases and sentences used frequently, like "Good morning," "Good day," "Good evening," "How are you?" helps to effect the carry-over.

Hearing yourself speak over an amplifying system is a boost to the carry-over because you hear yourself as you speak and an automatic correction occurs. Many tape-recording machines have this added feature.

Dictionary practice is good for carry-over of easy attack of vowels. Take the "a, e, i, o, u" words. Begin a sentence with each word.

If you have difficulty thinking up talking practice, read a story, a newspaper article, a section in an encyclopedia, and then recall aloud what you have read. Listen to a radio newscast and then say aloud what you remember of it. Watch a television show, switch it off, and immediately talk about it. Practice! Practice! Happy voices!

Chapter XIII

Vocal Problems and What
to Do about Them

All of the exercises you have been doing will make your voice pleasant. Even more importantly, they will improve the health of your voice and help prevent many physical problems of the vocal cords. A great many physical conditions are caused by vocal abuse alone and these can be alleviated by doing the exercises.

However, since there are also some physical disabilities which need medical or surgical attention, you must first go to your throat specialist if you have any of the following physical symptoms: hoarseness, tightening of the larynx or surrounding area, tiredness in the throat, cracks in the voice, loss of voice, loss of range, loss of volume, weakness, voice breaks, in singers the loss of the ability to sing softly but not loudly, or the onset of a tremolo.

In many instances, your throat specialist will tell you no medical treatment is necessary, and if medical or surgical treatment is necessary, do the exercises afterward. The chances are good that you have simply been misusing your voice and the exercises will offer help. But I do reiterate—go to your throat specialist first. When a patient who has been hoarse comes to me I will not even treat him until after he has been to the throat specialist for a check-up.

Those disorders, which can be prevented by the exercises and alleviated by them after medical or surgical treatment, are:

Simple inflamation and swelling of the cords, without infection.

Vocal nodules: singer's nodes, kissing nodes, corns, small protuberance on one or both vocal cords, always at the site of one-third of the way back from the front and the vocal cords.

Polyps: a smooth tumor projecting from the vocal cords at any site and at varying sizes.

Polypoid corditis: inflammatory tumors.

Thickening of the vocal cords: generalized thickening.

Contact ulcer granuloma: kissing ulcers, ulceration always at the posterior part of one vocal cord and sometimes at the point directly opposite on the other vocal cord. The piling up of particles falling from the ulcer forms the granuloma in the bed of the ulcer.

Hematoma: a localized hemorrhage in a vocal cord projecting like a small tumor.

These disorders are caused by a combination of all the factors we have described in the book:

faulty breathing, abrupt manner of initiating tone, speaking or singing at the wrong pitch, limited melody range, excessive strain in the use of volume, excessive tension in the larynx. The exercises are designed to correct this.

The rules we asked you to follow in Chapter II are important, too, for physical reasons as well as for improving sound. For instance:

Whenever you clear your throat or cough or laugh very hard, the vocal folds hit violently together and become irritated. After repeated clearing, coughing, or hard laughing, instead of remaining white they become pink and even red. This may also cause a hematoma or a burst blood vessel. Much of this clearing is a habit, but it can be overcome. Often a patient will say he can't possibly stop clearing his throat. He is surprised, however, when after one or two weeks he can eliminate a good deal, if not all of it. As we said in Chapter I, swallow instead of clearing. If you still have excess mucous, blow on an "h" sound, pant, or squeeze it up. If you absolutely must clear, do it without voice, as clearing hard with voice is the most harmful.

Another important rule is the one on silence during infectious laryngitis.

If you strain your voice during the acute phase, you may damage your vocal cords. For, during laryngitis, the vocal cords are swollen and inflamed, and this prevents them from elongating, causing low pitch, as the shorter the vocal cords, the lower the pitch. You are then not only talking with too low a pitch, but you are straining; because, to put your cords into vibration, there must be an extra push of air. This results in an excessive tightening of the muscles. When you talk with laryngitis, these bad habits become permanent even after the infection disappears, and the strain often leads to vocal nodules, polyps, and thickening of the vocal cords. So, if you're a housewife, stop talking to your children for a day. If you're a salesman, give up a day.

The following examples will show you what can happen if you don't heed this warning. A young woman, a publicity director for a large publishing house, went to Paris on her vacation, encountered cold and rainy weather, and came down with infectious laryngitis. Since she wanted to make the most of every moment, she continued visiting and sightseeing and—to make matters worse—practicing her French, thus creating even more tension. When she returned to New York, she had much work involving phone calls, meetings with authors and editors and so on, and strained her voice more and more until she could barely talk. At this point she consulted a throat specialist, who saw polyps in her throat which by now had grown too large to be reduced by vocal therapy alone. He operated and then prescribed complete silence for two weeks, forbidding whispering as well as talking.

The silence was necessary because the vocal cords come together and vibrate even when a single word is uttered. Just as you wouldn't knock the inner sides of your knees together if they were injured, you should never knock your vocal cords together while they are healing.

After so many months of straining her voice while she had laryngitis, the young lady's voice needed re-educating. Her pitch had spiraled downward two notes, from talking during the laryngitis. We raised her pitch, and she proceeded to do the exercises at her new level. She even went so far as to blow her pitch pipe each time she answered the telephone. Thus, the habit carried more quickly into everyday living. She told me with humor, however, that she didn't go so far as to blow it during business conferences.

She was assiduous in doing her exercises. She did them five minutes each morning, and during the course of the day stopped every few hours and did them for two minutes.

After a month, she decreased to once daily for five minutes every morning, and finally in six months was able to stop completely. Now her voice is melodious, easy, and relaxed, and it has become a valuable asset in her business and personal life.

Another patient, an actor, called from New York where he was in a play. He had just come from his doctor, who told him he had infectious laryngitis but no growth. "What do I do?" he asked. I said, "You know what to do. Cancel tonight. Remain on silence one to two days until the infection has cleared." "I know, I know," he said, "but I'm an actor. There is no understudy. No one can play my part." He went on stage that night and his hoarse voice lasted to the final curtain. The next day his doctor observed his vocal cords. The infection was gone, but there was a swelling at the ante-

rior third part of each vocal cord, the typical beginning of vocal nodules. Just one day of silence would
have cleared up his laryngitis, and his vocal cords
would have been in perfect condition, but now he
was in trouble. We went to work. The high pitches
of his range, typical of vocal nodules, were excessively breathy, hoarse, and strained. His middle
pitches were clear and easy. His low pitches were
hoarse. We went through the most difficult lines of
the play and eliminated the high and low pitches
and kept the melody variations for expression in his
middle range.

He kept his role keyed at his good middle
pitch level until his vocal cords returned to normal,
when he was able to add more pitches with ease.
So he had immediate help in overcoming the vocal
misuse, and the protuberances subsided in two
weeks. However, if he had gone on misusing the
voice, they would have increased and become
fibrous.

We have stressed the need for complete silence during the acute phase of infectious laryngitis,
for the two to three weeks following surgery, and
after an episode of acute vocal strain. This silence
should not be carried to such extremes, however,
that it will cause emotional problems.

I had one patient, for example, who had a
contact ulcer of the larynx which showed no sign
of diminishing. His doctor had recommended silence until the ulcer was completely healed, and for
three months my patient hadn't uttered a word. He

had been doing something just as harmful, which
defeated the whole purpose of silence. He was constantly clearing his throat, and thus his vocal cords
were hitting together violently right on the ulcer.
The patient was in a state of increasing tension because of his extreme need to talk. We call this a
form of subvocal speech.

Our first step was to show him how to counteract this tension by being aware of the tightened
feeling on the throat, the feeling of a closed throat,
and by showing him how to relax his throat by
breathing deeply. A week later, his doctor was won
over to the use of vocal therapy when he saw the
first sign of a decrease in the ulcer's size. The doctor
realized that gentle vocal exercise at a higher pitch
might help heal the ulcer, as it stretches the vocal
cords so that the indentation of the ulcer disappears
much as a notch in a rubber band does when it is
stretched. This was proved by the research done at
Northwestern University, and one can see it in
their ultra-high motion pictures of the vocal cords.

The patient came to see me again and began
to pull out his pad. "Go ahead and talk." I told him,
"I have to hear you to know what's wrong, and then
we can change it." "Wow!" He beamed. "Do you
really mean it?" During the first week of treatment
he remained in partial silence and practiced his exercises five minutes of each hour, coming in for an
hour lesson daily, during which time he talked in
his new voice under guidance. The second week he
continued the lessons and talked all he wanted to

except out-of-doors and above noise. A month later, when he went back to his doctor for his check-up, the ulcer had completely disappeared.

Thus, we feel that prolonged silence lasting more than three weeks is unnecessary, provided you alter the way you are using the voice and remove those factors which irritate the vocal cords. Naturally, the best way to do this is under the guidance of a qualified vocal therapist, but if this is impossible, this book should help you correct the use of your voice.

If you do have a vocal problem similar to those we have described in this chapter, avoid milk as well as beer, as they create additional mucus in the throat, which in turn causes more throat clearing.

Lozenges, gargles and sprays may give temporary relief to feelings of vocal fatigue or soreness, but prolong vocal difficulties. It is better to feel the irritation and, consequently, use the voice easier. Medication should be used only through a physician's recommendation and only for specific infections.

Some people believe the cause of their vocal problems is a deviated nasal septum or a post nasal drip. These may aggravate the problem, but are not causative and do not prevent vocal betterment.

The chapter on easy initiating is most important for sound and is also important because one of the main factors in causing ulcer, polyps, etc., is the banging together of the vocal cords roughly instead of gently. Since this involves the glottal area, we call this the "glottal plosive attack."

When you start a word with a vowel, you either slip into the tone easily and softly, or you begin sharply and abruptly. If you do the latter when you initiate tone, especially in words beginning with vowels *or* an "M" or "N," you are doing irreparable damage to your vocal cords. Instead of bringing them together tenderly and gently, you are banging them together like cymbals clashing together in an orchestra. Your vocal cords can't withstand this, for they aren't made of durable metal but of soft tissue, and constant friction and banging is ruinous to them.

The relaxing exercises which help excessive tension of the larynx are important not only for sound, but in the prevention of many physical problems. When there is extreme tension one may develop a condition of forcing the false vocal cords, which are above the true cords, to come together and vibrate. Normally, they stay in back and play no part in the production of voice. When they do come together and vibrate, an extremely deep and raucous voice results.

When your pitch is too low, thus making the voice sound rough, it also irritates the vocal cords and is one of the causes of an ulceration, as a contact ulcer always occurs at this back part of the vocal cords where the rubbing takes place. The rubbing stops instantly when you come up to a clear pitch level.

The growths we have talked about so far are usually caused by vocal abuse. By following the exercises in this book, you will avoid such abuses. If you have had any one of the growths, follow the exercises even more carefully, for there is the possibility of a return of the growth. Contact ulcers, for instance, return very quickly and repeatedly unless the abuses are eliminated.

Now we come to those disorders which are not caused by vocal misuse. Needless to say, these are completely and solely within the province of the throat specialist. However, the exercises will help your voice after medical correction by a specialist.

When one vocal cord has been removed completely, the voice must be brought back very gently and slowly to gain the best possible quality without force. If one of the vocal cords is removed, a fairly normal voice can be obtained by early vocal therapy so that the good vocal cord can be brought over gently to vibrate against the scar tissue on the opposite side. This generally can be done in two or three lessons if carried out immediately after the three-weeks' silence following the operation and before strain has set in by the person forcing his voice back.

When the entire larynx is removed, one must learn a new way of producing voice, by belching. Training for this type of voice involves a greater scope than presented in this book. Some people whose larynx has been removed do not bother to improve the sound of their new voice produced on the belches rather than the vocal cords. They often sound low and belchy and monotonous. It is possible for them to improve the sound, develop melody, and even sing. The singing is not beautiful with esophageal voice, but the speaking voice can become pleasing by practicing the exercises in this book. Mainly, these people should work on the chapters in gaining resonance, pitch, and melody. An elevation in pitch alone makes the voice sound remarkably better. Diction as well as vocal exercises are necessary. This and other aspects are covered completely in the excellent book, *Speech Rehabilitation of the Laryngectomized,* by John C. Snidecor and others, Charles C Thomas, Publisher, Springfield, Illinois.

Once the individual is able to belch he can improve the tone and naturalness of the voice by carrying out the exercises in Chapters 9, 10, and 11.

An extremely deep pitch is usually obtained when a person begins talking on the belches. I have found these voices to be more pleasant when the pitch is raised and melody is added. It is entirely possible to do this once the person can keep the belches coming voluntarily and the exercises give more vocal control. I have them start singing up in pitch on such words as "me," "may," "my," and gradually increase range and do all the melody work. If they cannot go up in this manner at first, they usually will be able to slide up.

Another disorder is paralysis of one vocal cord. One cause of this is a severance of a nerve, sometimes following a thyroid operation. A skillful surgeon always looks for the recurrent laryngeal nerve and makes sure it is out of the way during the surgery in a thyroid operation. Sometimes, however, it is so deeply imbedded that it is impossible to save this nerve, resulting in paralyzed vocal cords which makes the voice breathy, as excess air escapes when the paralysis prevents closure. In the bilateral case two vocal cords are affected with the possible result of no voice, only whispering. There is corrective surgery for this condition, after which, with vocal therapy, these people can attain a fairly clear voice—sometimes completely clear. If this unfortunate thing happens, the exercises will restore the voice to its maximum improvement.

One young woman was seen with her vocal cords in this state but with only one vocal cord affected. She had lost her singing voice and spoke in a hoarse, breathy tone. With therapy, the normal vocal cord was able to come over beyond the midline and meet the vocal cord that wasn't functioning because of the paralyzed muscle. She recovered her singing voice and speaking voice within a month. This recovery was unusual, however, for in most similar cases it takes much longer—six months, perhaps. A recent surgical procedure has helped certain unilateral vocal cord paralyses. This is an injection of teflon into the affected cord, which automatically improves the voice. This treatment has been developed by Dr. Godfrey E. Arnold.

Another organic condition occurs when one cord is congenitally shorter than the other vocal cord. One boy who was seen had a hoarse voice all his life and came for therapy at the age of eighteen. He worked diligently on breath control, the humming type of exercises, and proper pitch placement, and was able to improve his voice. And, although it was not completely normal, it was clearer and carried more than it had before.

There are also vocal problems which result solely from emotional causes in which the vocal cords are normal.

One type of vocal problem which is recognized fully on an emotional basis is called "hysterical aphonia." This is a complete loss of voice with no organic cause. A severe case of this kind was brought into the in-patient psychiatric department of a hospital. The patient was a woman who had not said one word, even a whisper, in four years. She had to write everything she wanted to say. She underwent intensive psychiatric treatment, but because psychotherapy depends on the patient's talking about their problems, they called me in first to get her voice back. Knowing that strong, positive suggestion helps in hysterical cases. I told her when I first went into her room that she just didn't have enough breath for a voice, and that she would work on getting this breath, enabling her to talk. I gave her a glass of water with a drinking tube from her side table and told her to blow bubbles into the water. She was not able to get one bubble through. I said, "See, you just don't have enough breath! If you can't get one bubble, you don't have enough breath coming over to set the vocal cords in vibration. You must practice blowing all weekend, and I'll come in on Monday; by Monday, you will have practiced blowing so much that you're going to blow bubbles into that tube—and then you will talk!"

I went back on Monday, and she took a deep breath and blew. She not only blew a few bubbles into the glass, she blew so hard that the water spattered all over the bed. I told her, "Now you have enough air to talk, so tell me your name." She struggled a bit and took a deep breath and said, "Ida." Then she said one word after another. Soon all the patients and doctors and nurses from the floor came into her room, and she named them all. She became the most talkative patient on the floor. If she had gone home immediately, it would only have been a matter of time until she would lose her voice again, but she stayed on for four months and had daily psychiatric treatment. The causes of her difficulties were determined and resolved. Then she returned home, undertook a new vocation, and ceased to be the completely dependent person she had been formerly in her complete escape from reality.

There is another type of vocal problem known as "hysterical dysphonia" and referred to an emotional difficulty with the voice which left it with a very strange, forced, strained type of voice with hoarseness. The condition is now called "spastic dysphonia," and it is different from the usual type of hoarseness; a complete tightening of the laryngeal muscles and sounds occurs, as if the person is crying in the throat. It presents great difficulty in overcoming, even through psychotherapy and vocal therapy. More recent investigations have shown that there is a neurological involvement for which no known cure is possible today. Mild cases, however, may be helped through training the voice. More severe cases of long duration can be helped only by using the voice with at least the most possible ease and preserving it with the least amount of strain, but it cannot become completely normal through exercising.

Chapter XIV

Stuttering and Other Disorders

The feeling of self-consciousness of those who stutter is out of proportion to their difficulty. This is due in large part to the unfortunate and unnecessary connotation society has put on the word "stutterer." When one who stutters realizes that this speech problem is not so grave, there is actually a lessening of the stuttering. Wendell Johnson, the great authority on stuttering, said that a certain tribe of Indians had no name for stuttering and consequently never had this problem.

The first step those who stutter must take is to realize he is not set apart from his fellow men, that he doesn't have to be self-conscious about his stuttering, and that he can lessen it by practice.

The father of one of my young patients told me that he had stuttered considerably until he was in action in World War II. When he suddenly realized how insignificant his stuttering was, he said he never stuttered from then on!

Sometimes the tightening up over stuttering can be lessened by using the pauses for greater effectiveness in speech. For instance, often a pause can bring out more meaning to the listener. Students in public speaking courses are often advised to do this. Winston Churchill often had long pauses in overcoming a block, which proved extremely effective.

A law student who came to me had been trying to hide his stuttering by avoiding difficult words, and groaned every time the word "terrible" slipped out. "Didn't you notice how long it took me to get out that word 'terrible'?" he asked. "I tightened up so inside that it took me forever." I told him that this tenseness was not apparent and often this pause before a word could be effective.

"Stuttering is so terrible," a thirty-year-old patient told me.

"Yes, it is to you, but not to others," I replied. He quickly rebutted, "Oh, but it is to others too. I can't stand to hear another person stutter." "That's *you*," I said. "You and others who stutter hate it. People who don't stutter don't condemn it as you do." A person with this difficulty can never stand it in others, and hearing another person block even brings on more trouble for both. About fifteen years ago an outstanding psychoanalyst and I brought together a group of ten men who stuttered. The effect was deadly. Instead of speaking freely to us as they had before individually, the men had tremendously increased trouble. Three dropped out of the group after the first session. Seven continued. Results were poor and the group was disbanded. It was concluded that individual therapy or group therapy with only one patient who stuttered was far better than with a group of stutterers. This is not true of people with other types of problems in speech. My groups of people with voice problems have benefited considerably, as have diction and other groups. But not stuttering!

"It's the way you people feel about yourselves and others with stuttering! If you didn't feel it was so bad, you wouldn't stutter as much."

"Gosh," he said, "I never thought of it that way. You know, you're right. When I was in college, I had a friend who stuttered. Whenever we were together, I stuttered much more than usual."

Many patients have come to me for their stuttering, and I sometimes have difficulty in detecting it. This is because they often skillfully substitute words to avoid those that give trouble. For instance, a law student in therapy for this condition had never spoken in class, and when he spoke on other occasions, he used this trick of substituting another word for the one he thought he might stutter on. Even I had difficulty in finding out when he blocked. When he began an all-out attack on this, ceased the substitutions, and began to talk in classes, I detected his stuttering easily. He was discouraged at first, as his speech seemed to get worse, but he understood the reason and pursued his improvement plan. Gradually he noticed improvement and was glad he had forced himself to correct his speech instead of avoiding the troublesome words.

There isn't anyone who doesn't have some difficulty when he starts tackling situations he has previously avoided. In the final analysis each person undergoing speech therapy or psychotherapy must go out and practice himself in order to improve. This applies to stutterers as well. A stutterer should therefore not avoid speaking, for the more he talks and practices speech improvement, the better off he will be. He should do this even if his stuttering seems to get worse at the beginning.

When one who stutters realizes he is entering new situations and gaining a little more freedom, he will develop more confidence and gradually feel less self-conscious about his stuttering.

With stuttering, I feel it is an emotional problem which often needs dynamic psychiatric treatment. I have worked with psychiatrists for eighteen years and know the benefits many of my patients have received from them. But sometimes a psychiatrist, referring a patient to me who stutters, will say, "This man has a good adjustment in his home and work life. I see no reason for tampering with his emotions, but he has a stutter which I wish you'd give your old speech try with." I've seen a good many adults with a reference like this and with them I use the chapters on Relaxation, Breathing, Easy Initiating, Melody and Volume. The latter two are especially beneficial. I use these also with children who stutter. The main idea behind them in reference to stuttering is to develop in them a joy of speech, a love of talking. Rarely do you encounter a person who stutters in singing. Giving more melody to speaking makes it easier to get the words out, and it becomes fun. As they learn they can improve, they develop more confidence and improve further. The more enjoyment and enthusiasm they build in talking, the less they stutter.

I've known physicians who, because they stuttered, chose research rather than private practice, but when they became outstanding in research, they were called upon to talk about it in teaching medical students and at meetings. They came to me for help. On their first visit I'd say to them, "But you can have such fun giving a talk. You can enjoy getting up before an audience." They'd stare back blankly, not believing me. For instance, a few months later, one man called excitedly, "I just returned from Chicago. My speech was great. Never had such fun in my life." It doesn't even mean they got over their stuttering, but they can learn to enjoy talking, face up to speaking situations and get through them. Naturally, I always tell them about Winston Churchill and how he stuttered so much through many a speech, yet became one of the world's greatest orators. Even when he gave great speeches, he still had blocks at times. So a direct attack on speech and development of melody may help a person who stutters to improve, even though it is not a cure.

Ideally, a person who stutters will have both speech and psychotherapy. There are times when the causes are determined and resolved and the stuttering remains. Here too, a direct attack on symptoms is beneficial.

Many exercises in this book will be helpful to those who stutter. It is usually easier to start with the simpler speaking situations before leading up to the harder ones. Begin with the word exercises and increase gradually to the poems and later to the most complex speaking situations, such as a public speech. As you desensitize yourself to the small situations, later you will go out in the world and find that your problem is not insurmountable.

Poems must be read aloud to be appreciated; they have a special value in speech practice. They have a rhythm and cadence and play of sounds which lend themselves to increased expression through melody. Take a poem you like and read it aloud ten times and more. Each time think of the meaning and of expressing it. Record it the first time you read it aloud and re-record it after reading it twenty-five times or a hundred times. You will have a fine before-and-after record if you have made a real effort. Each time you read the poem, tune up first with one of the vocal exercises in scale form in your range. This will give you the pitch flexibility. Then use all these pitches in reading the poem aloud. Think of using all the pitches and using melody for your expression, and of bringing out meaning through your expression. It will give you confidence to hear how pleasing you can sound.

The chapter on increasing loudness is especially helpful to those who stutter, as it affords a release of hostility. A build-up of hostility will increase the problem. Even though stuttering may be an emotional problem needing psychiatric treatment, there are tricks which can help. Sometimes I ask patients to keep track of each small annoyance and bring me a list of them. They recount these to me and feel better afterward. Naturally, we never delve deeply as a psychiatrist does; a speech therapist may do harm in tampering with the unconscious. However, we can help to some extent by not allowing these small irritations to add up to one big hostile reaction by handling them day to day as they occur. It's a lot easier, too, to say something at the time to the person who annoyed you. It may be said simply and politely. Daily living is then more pleasant and speech becomes easier.

Practice the increase in volume. Make up situations from real life that bother you. Shout at your spouse. Scream at your boss. Have fun, and you'll stutter less. I met a man one day recently who had been a patient of mine as a child of eight. When you grow up and try to recall what went on in therapy at the age of eight, you don't remember much. He said the one thing he remembered was that I had had him shout out a bunch of swear words, and he was convinced that was what relieved him of his stuttering. This is actually a helpful device with children. I tell them there's this game we may play here, but he can't play it with his mother or his father or anyone else. He knows full well that his mother told him not to curse and he can't use it in polite company. But here he finds the approval of an adult who understands him, it frees him of some of the hostility, and he feels good about it. In turn, this reduces his speech blocks.

The mother of a high school senior called me recently and complained, "Laddie isn't practicing. I don't hear him. You told me not to keep after him, but shouldn't he be practicing?"

My answer was, "He is carrying out his assignments. We have reached a different stage now which does not include direct speech practice. He has assignments which he does carry out, as he has to report to me about them. His reports have been excellent."

"Oh." The mother seemed relieved. "I wondered why he sounded so much better without practicing."

I did not discuss the assignments with her because these were between Laddie and me. All therapy should be confidential. Laddie's current assignment was to make small remarks to the person who annoyed him. His list grew and grew. He never wrote them down. They were in his head, he'd tell me, and he did relate many incidents. He managed to do it politely with his parents and teachers and no one took offense as he thought they would. This in itself gives one a feeling of confidence. He accepted the fact that everything is not perfect all the time and that sometimes he'd have a day when he stuttered more. One day, for instance, his German teacher demanded that he repeat a question ten times. Each time he stuttered more. Finally the teacher understood him, but he felt self-conscious and it was a week before he could muster up enough courage to speak again in any class. Then he bounced back and was in the swing of self-improvement again.

You must take the downs with the ups and keep on trying. If you try long and hard enough, you'll have failures, but you'll also have successes. There is no success without trying. As Theodore Roosevelt said in his speech before the Hailton Club, Chicago (April 10, 1900):

> Far better it is to dare mighty things, to win glorious triumphs, even though checkered by failure, than to take rank with those poor spirits who neither enjoy much nor suffer much, because they live in the gray twilight that knows not victory nor defeat.

I find that those who stutter take delight in developing their voices to their fullest potential. Any improvement in speech gives them more confidence. One young man was extremely self-belittling at first, and afraid to talk. My notes from the first interview with him were as follows:

"He blocked so severely at times that he gave up the attempt. He spelled out many words. He kept away from the telephone and never spoke in or to groups. His fear of speaking before a group was so great, he had left school at sixteen because of it."

Yet he eventually developed a resonant voice. At twenty-four he earned his high school diploma, left Philadelphia to study dramatics. He called me from New York not long ago when he got his first good acting job. His voice sounded marvelous, even better than when I had seen him last four years previously. He said he had continued the vocal exercises every day.

Those who stutter will find great help from the books of Van Riper, Johnson, and others (see Bibliography).

All the work in the book will help the voices of the hard-of-hearing if they are able to hear by means of hearing-aid amplification, even though they do need extra work in auditory training. They must learn to hear some pitch differentiation. They may not be able to carry a tune or sing exact notes, but they can improve their speech melody and quality of voice. Of course, they also need diction work which is not included in this book. Diction concerns the proper articulation of speech sound and we need not be concerned with it throughout this book, as it has little to do with improvement of the voice.

The person with cleft palate needs diction work, but may improve voice through all the chapters. In addition to the voice work here, these people need to lessen nasality, which they may do through concentrating on the quality heard on vowels in Chapter 8. The vowels are the sounds which carry the excessive nasality. By opening the mouth wider and directing the áir out of the mouth, less nasality is heard. The "h" sounds help relieve nasality. A good deal of practice with the exercises in this chapter helps relieve nasality.

Bibliography

Brodnitz, Friedrich S.: *Vocal Rehabilitation.* Rochester, Minnesota, American Academy of Ophthalmology & Otolaryngology, 1959.

Bryngelson, B., M. Chapman, and O. Hanson: *Know Yourself: A Workbook for Those Who Stutter.* Minneapolis, Burgess Publishing Co., 1944.

Eisenson, J.: *The Improvement of Voice and Diction.* New York, The Macmillan Company, 1958.

English, O. S., and G. H. J. Pearson: *Emotional Problems of Living.* Third edition. New York, W. W. Norton & Co. Inc., 1963.

Greene, Margaret C. L.: *The Voice and Its Disorders.* New York, The Macmillan Company, 1957.

Hahn, E., C. W. Lomas, D. E. Hargis, and D. Vandraegen: *Basic Voice Training.* New York, McGraw-Hill, 1958.

Jackson, C., and C. L. Jackson: *Diseases of the Nose, Throat and Ear.* Second edition. Philadelphia, W. B. Saunders Co., 1959.

Johnson, W.: "An Open Letter to the Mother of a Stuttering Child, You and Your Child." Reprinted in *Journal of Speech and Hearing Disorders,* 14 (1949), 3-8.

———— (editor): *Stuttering in Children and Adults.* Minneapolis, University of Minnesota Press, 1955.

Levin, Nathaniel M.: *Voice and Speech Disorders: Medical Aspects.* Springfield, Ill., Charles C Thomas, Publisher, 1962.

Negus, V. E.: *The Mechanism of the Larynx.* London, William Heineman, Ltd., 1929.

Schreiber, F. R.: *Your Child's Speech.* New York, G. P. Putnam's Sons, 1956.

Snidecor, John C.: *Speech Rehabilitation of the Laryngectomized.* Springfield, Ill., Charles C Thomas, Publisher, 1962.

Travis, Edward, and others: *Handbook of Speech Pathology.* New York, Appleton-Century-Crofts, 1957.

Von Leden, Hans, and Paul Moore: *Contact Ulcer— New Observations on Etiology and Therapy Processes.* Sixth International Congress of Otolaryngology, 1957.

Van Riper, C.: *Speech Correction: Principles and Methods.* Fourth edition. Englewood Cliffs, N.J.: Prentice-Hall, Inc., 1963.

————, and John V. Irwin: *Voice and Articulation.* Englewood Cliffs, N.J., Prentice-Hall, Inc., 1958.